QUANTUM PROFITS

To Mark,
I literally could not have completed our last job without you
Bob

QUANTUM PROFITS

SAVING WESTERN MANUFACTURING
USING THE FOURTH DIMENSION

WILLIAM CHAMBLESS

Copyright © 2012 by William Chambless.

Library of Congress Control Number: 2012904646
ISBN: Hardcover   978-1-4691-8308-4
              Softcover   978-1-4691-8307-7
              Ebook   978-1-4691-8309-1

All rights reserved. No part of this book may be reproduced or transmitted in any form or by any means, electronic or mechanical, including photocopying, recording, or by any information storage and retrieval system, without permission in writing from the copyright owner.

This book was printed in the United States of America.

To order additional copies of this book, contact:
Xlibris Corporation
1-888-795-4274
www.Xlibris.com
Orders@Xlibris.com
107952

CONTENTS

Introduction 11
    Is it a Scary World?.. 11
    Time: The Fourth Dimension 11
    Design and Response Are Key... 12
    Stories to Illustrate Theory... 13

Chapter 1:   Before You Plan.. 15
    Start with Purpose 15
    Opportunity Crossing Preparations.. 16
    Invent Your Reality.. 16
    Instill a Vision 17
    Follow the Money.. 17
    Think Small... 18

Chapter 2:   Plan 19
    Establish a Five-Year Plan That Everyone
        Can Be Passionate About... 19
    Beyond the Hedgehog Concept 19
    Define Year 5 in Profitability and Market Share 20
    Reverse Engineer Years 1 through 5 21
    Focusing on Time, Purpose, Design, and
        Thinking Small Does Fit Together... 21

Chapter 3:   Execution 22
    Planning Starts Top Down 22
    Long View.. 23

Drill Down to Year 1 24
Goals 24
Cellular Organizations 24
Team Metrics 25

Chapter 4: Mass versus Short-Run Responsive
            Production and Services 29

Chapter 5: Understand the Dynamics of Improvement: Part 1 33
Variation Is the Enemy 33
Single-Piece Flow Increases Throughput
    and Reduces Footprints 34
Biggest Opportunity to Reduce Lead
    Times Is to Reduce White Space 37
Cellular Operations 39
Focus on Dramatically Reducing Lead Times
    and Not On-Time Deliveries 40
Conversely, Focus on Lead Times to Dramatically
    Improve Overall Percent of On-time Deliveries 41
Focus on Keeping People and Equipment
    Busy Leads to Wrong Decisions 41
Do Not Misplace Compassion 42

Chapter 6: Understand the Dynamics of Improvement: Part 2 43
Focusing on Efficiency for Short-Run
    Operations is Counterproductive 43
Look to Operations to Increase Capacity
    before Spending Money 45
Theory of Constraints 45
    Joe the Plumber and TOC 46
    Joe's First Attempt Failed 47
    Joe the Plumber's TOC Solution:
        Increase Joe's Capacity to Perform the Other Duties 48
Take Multiple Buffers Away from Projects 49
Don't Multitask 50
    1. Impact on pending projects 51
    2. Need to reorient or remobilize between tasks 51
    3. Clutter causing wasted movement 51

    4. Loss of insight 52
    5. Opportunity loss 52
    6. Little's law 53

Chapter 7: Reset Operations 54
  Scheduler's Responsibility and Authority 54
  Manufacturing Team's Responsibility and Authority 55
  Shipping Team's Responsibility and Authority 56
  Plant Engineer's Responsibility and Authority 56
  Plant Manager's Responsibility and Authority 57

Chapter 8: Use A3 Thinking 58
  The Way We Think and A3 Thinking 59
  An Example of A3: Assess Way Forward to Reduce Lead Times 59
  A3 Title: Reduce average lead-times from eight to four days 59
    Current Condition 59
    Goals/Targets 60
    Analysis (Root Causes) 60
    Countermeasures 60
    Plan 61
    Follow-up 62

Chapter 9: 5Ss 63
  Seri—Sort 64
  Seiton—Set in Order 65
  Seiso—Sweep 66
  Seiketsu—Standardize 67
  Shitsuki—Sustain 67

Chapter 10: Kaizen Events 68

Chapter 11: Behavioral Change 73
  Push Through the Valley of Despair 73
  Change Individual Behavior by Addressing
    Why We Resist Change 73
  Be a Player, Not a Victim 75
  Increase Time Spent on Change 76
  Settle for the Doable Rather than the Most Logical 77

  Conscientiously Incorporate a Mechanism for
   Continuous Improvement 77

Chapter 12: Problem Solving 79
  Five Whys 82
   Examples of Five Whys 82
  Tools to Solve Complex Problems: Speak with Data 84
  Get an Assist from the Right Brain 85
  Sometimes Simple is a Magical Cure 87
  Solve Problems and Quality from the Front End 88
  Change Our Culture from Accepting Problems
   to Solving Problems as They Arise 89

Chapter 13: Guide to Prosperity 92

INDEX 95

Endnotes 99

The business fourth dimension "time" drives quality, cost, and volume. Small to midsize businesses must compete by being flexible, and responsive. They must see time as a competitive weapon. Time trumps traditional views on people and capacity utilization. Shortening lead times not only wins customers, but improving processes has near-magical effects on all business metrics. "Quantum Profits" moves beyond methodology and discusses solutions in real small and midsize businesses. It is a "must read" for companies stuggling to find a new profitable direction.

INTRODUCTION

Is it a Scary World?

I have had the opportunity to rebuild over twenty companies over the past thirty years. I watched companies evolve from bloated behemoths with layers of management to devouring tigers. In 2005 Thomas Friedman warned in *The Word Is Flat: A Brief History of the Twenty-First Century* that telecommunications have exposed the West to competitors having vast engineering and programming skills.[1] We now outsource telemarketing, accounting, computer programming, engineering, and scientific research, etc.; Friedman predicted that mass manufacturing will continue to move offshore. Does this mean our standards of living will flatten to a low level? Not necessarily. In 2011 we saw signs of US manufacturing returning.[2] Manufacturing exports to China and Brazil increased from 2010 to 2011 during the great recession. John Deere and Caterpillar hired more people in the midwest and southwest. Ironically, employment in high-skilled manufacturing jobs in the United States soared between 1983 and 2003, the era about which Friedman wrote.[3] John Deere announced repatriation of one of its foreign operations to two factories in Iowa. Average computer numerical control machine operator in the industrial Ohio earns $75,000 per year. Jobs go unfilled. How can this be?

Time: The Fourth Dimension

Quantum theory extended and contradicted traditional thinking. $E = mc^2$ exploded our understanding of energy contained in small units of matter. Time is the component in the conceptual age that unlocks the energy in fast-growth businesses. Toyota taught us that reducing cycle time has a positive impact on quality and costs. They pioneered SMED or single-minute exchange of die. SMED revolutionized the car industry. Manufacturers no longer had to run thousands of cars because of costly changeovers. From 1995 to 2005, the number of models of cars and trucks sold in the United States rose from 910 to 1590. Online capabilities cut the stranglehold of the establishment. Future companies must be nimble and anticipate customer demand. Steve Jobs revolutionized the world by seemly divining future lifestyles. The cornerstone of traditional western liberal thinking is "what can be." We must think small. We cannot overcommit to inflexible factories or staff.

Design and Response Are Key

We changed the way we viewed daily life in the Industrial Age. Rather than abandon agriculture, we made agriculture more productive. In the Conceptual Age, we must not abandon our base industries but make manufacturing more responsive and anticipatory. Ford's adage "You can have any color you want as long as it is black" is no longer viable. The West can no longer compete with commodity production. Daniel Pink, in discussing the Conceptual Age, points out that we are in the age of abundance.[4] People expect "thin," "beauty," and "plug-in and use". Japan, then Korea, took over commodity electronics; China is next in line. Why would Apple spend money to develop Apple TV? While as of February 2012, we do not know the specifics on the third generation of Apple TV, rumors suggest Apple is in talks with media executives at several large companies and is developing a TV with wireless streaming capabilities. Google recently jumped into Streaming TVs with Japanese and Korean TV manufacturers. Could this be an example of bringing control of television production back to the United States? Streaming programs are becoming ubiquitous on multiple devices. The West's response to its loss in dominance in the Information Age must be to refocus on design and rapid response. Ultimately, we must bring back manufacturing and services. Mastering short-run production to meet ever-changing demand has to be an integral component of our future strategy.

Stories to Illustrate Theory

I use stories to illustrate lessons from a lifetime dedicated to making improvements. I use several industries, in both manufacturing and services, to illustrate the universality of the concepts. Most improvements are incremental, not revolutionary. I encountered total quality management (TQM) in 1980, having spent several months in a Nissan factory in Japan. I was shocked that at the time, few people in the United States knew of W. Edwards Deming or Taiichi Ohno or other pioneers in modern manufacturing technology. That changed as Asian companies effectively dislodged the consumer electronics industry from the United States in the 1970s and 1980s and were making a similar run at our auto industry. The United States finally responded by adopting Toyota technology and domestically developing what we know today as Six Sigma. While I used many of the concepts in Six Sigma over the years, I only formally received my certificate of Lean Six Sigma Master Black Belt in 2010 from Villanova University. Over the last thirty-two years, I have had an opportunity to help improve operations at billion-dollar corporations and multiple small to midsize businesses. Further, I have used Quick Response Manufacturing that Dr. Rajan Suri discussed in his book, *Quick Response Manufacturing: A Companywide Approach to Reducing Lead Times*, published in 1998.[5] I had many jobs at Gulf, Chevron and CONOCO, from research chemist to business manager for specialty chemicals. I left the corporate world to develop multiple companies in 1986. We grew companies from below ten million dollars to up to six hundred million dollars. There are many books written about billion-dollar corporations, but few about small to midsize companies.

I thought of calling this book *Secrets from a Lifelong Consultant*. I share what has been successful for me at hundreds of consulting opportunities. I have a strong background in statistics and methodology though this book focuses on application. Please follow up on references or e-mail me at bill@williamchambless.com for additional details on methodology. I have seen thirty-year employees make the same mistakes thousands of times over the years. Rather than berating those thirty-year employees, we encourage employees to find solutions. We change cultures. The best practices are useless if we lack discipline. We discuss easing resistance to change. We emphasize the need to use all resources. Business is sometimes about keeping towns alive or supporting your in-laws. We explore how to be compassionate and serve our community, our employees, and our family.

CHAPTER 1

Before You Plan

Start with Purpose

Companies cannot afford *Fields of Dreams*. If you build a large factory or network today, and you are overcommitted to infrastructure, you are a dinosaur. Build on a purpose. Think of the most successful people or companies that you know and ask yourself, "Does their core purpose have their fingerprints over every aspect of their being?"

Purpose motivates. Ronald Reagan was defined by "morning in America"; Dr. Martin Luther King was defined by "I have a dream." Successful companies exude purpose. Walt Disney, "to make people happy," Walmart, "to give ordinary folk the chance to buy the same things as rich people" and Apple Computer, "Everything we do, we believe in challenging the status quo. We believe in thinking differently." Not only do the owners believe it, but their employees and customers believe. Everyone is comfortable buying computers, iPads, iPods, or iPhones from Apple. Purpose drives attitude, attitude drives behavior, and purposeful behavior drives success.

According to Simon Sinek, it is actually biology.[6] The human brain is broken into three major components. The neocortex processes the "what" level. It is responsible for all of our rational and analytical thoughts and language. The middle two sections make up our limbic brains. Our limbic brains are responsible for all of our feelings, like trust and loyalty. It is also responsible for all human behavior, all decision-making, and it has no capacity for language.

Facts do not drive behavior. *Purpose leads to trust and loyalty.* Purpose is why employees come to work, investors give us money, and customers buy.

Opportunity Crossing Preparations

In *Outliers: The Story of Success,* Malcolm Gladwell cites cases where extraordinary success takes more than extraordinary talent or extraordinary IQs. Success is most often achieved when people with sufficient, but not always extraordinary, talent or IQs have worked on their craft for at least ten thousand hours, and were born or were in the perfect place to take advantage of unique opportunities.[6] He cites Bill Gates and Bill Joy as having had unique opportunities to have nearly unlimited direct access to programming, while their contemporaries shared brief moment in a queue of card readers. I was an unfortunate "contemporary." When microcomputer hardware came of age, those few seasoned programmers could exploit new opportunities. Most people know Bill Gates's story. Bill Joy was one of four founders of Sun Microsystems and was responsible for most of the computer languages used nearly thirty years since. Indeed, as Gladwell points out, major contributors to the Information Age were born between 1953 and 1956. Pioneers include Bill Gates, 1955; Paul Allen, 1953; Steve Balmer, 1956; and Steve Jobs, 1955. Each had honed their skills with more than ten thousand hours of hard work before exploiting their opportunities.

Henry Hartman said, "Success always comes when preparation meets opportunities." In cases cited above, people with sufficient talent and IQs followed their passion and were prepared when opportunity arose. Most often, successful people are at the right place at the right time. There are but few examples of people truly creating opportunity. Steve Jobs, if any one, could be that exception. Asked if he wanted to do market research, he said, "No, because customers don't know what they want until we've shown them."[7]

Invent Your Reality

We are responsible. We can choose to be a player or victim. I have been on several sports champion teams and champion businesses. Mostly we inherited legacies of failure. We were winners when we decided to be winners.

As a chemist fresh from the lab, Gulf Oil assigned a business to me. My "grand prize" had barely made a profit in twenty years. Our competitor built three new plants that had a combined capacity four times larger, produced better quality products, and had better control of production. Our process generated hard-to-sell by-products. Our ability to sell by-products limited production. Our competitor, on the other hand, could "dial in" their product distribution. The previous managers sold commodities. Gulf reported our sales in barrels. As a manager with no managerial experience, I shocked the plant manager when I told him to open the plant full throttle. We loaded liquefied gases and waxes in rail cars and sent them off without homes. My sales people had to place product quickly at any price. The wax would solidify in five days. We convinced new specialty buyers that our product was acceptable, and we would give them better service than the "big guy." We used our technical skills to improve our customers' businesses and charged a premium. We sold product in quarts and drums. Over time, we cancelled comfortable, but marginal, commodity contracts. The business went from one of the worst in Gulf (later Chevron) to the most profitable on a return on sales or return on investment basis and remained so for four years. We bested our competitor on these same bases. We did not accept inferiority. We invented a new reality. I never did figure out how to convert drums to barrels.

Instill a Vision

Whatever you decide to be as a company, communicate in the present tense. You are not just laying bricks; you are building a community. Look beyond your current product or service. In the 1970s, Boeing bet the company on a radically new plane, the 747. More recently, Apple placed their bets on markets it created: iPhones, iPads, and in the future, iTV. Not only did they create reality, they were prepared to cannibalize their current popular products.

Follow the Money

Everyone agrees that 2008, 2009, and 2010 presented the worse economics in decades. Some companies made it big. It was not always the headline companies. The oil and gas industry boomed over these years. Was it better to be an exploration company or a sell auto parts? The growth was in parts. In bad times, people kept their clunkers rolling. The point is, look for the money.

Think Small

Expect fantastic, but think small in execution. Outsource to minimize capital. Build your success model before committing to infrastructure. Spend on flexible equipment over buildings and people. Use single-piece flow to minimize footprints. Keep shop floors and office desks free of work in progress and finished inventory. Move production out the door. Turn over investments in receivables and inventory as often as possible.

Chapter 2

Plan

Establish a Five-Year Plan That Everyone Can Be Passionate About

Start with purpose. State who you are so that financiers, suppliers, customers, and employees "get it." Steve Jobs was Apple. I have experienced two leaders that personified purpose or lack of purpose. One led our company from £50,000,000 to £400,000,000 in five years. John Hollowood inspired us in year 1 that INSPEC Group PLC would build our small fine chemical business to be a world-class competitor. It was five magical years. It reminded me of sports teams that defied the odds. We had a charismatic leader. The company was sold for one billion US dollars. The successor company's first five-year plan described success as laying-off 10 percent of their personnel per annum. Which company do you think was the most successful? Passion remains a prerequisite in the Conceptual Age.

Beyond the Hedgehog Concept

Jim Collins in *Good to Great* describes three components required to be "great."[8] We start with passion. Collins suggests two other components: The second, what can we be the best at? The third, can we be profitable? If you lack key talent, buy it. Look for passion—someone who has put in his or her ten thousand hours of dedication. Look for overachievers. The son of a wealthy family finishing at the top of his class is less impressive than a daughter who earned every penny of her college costs and still excelled. Profitability is the third component. While profitability is important, it cannot be the source of passion.

Some of the great companies that survived the Industrial and Information Ages must change in the Conceptual Age. Notable examples of companies that were great in 2001, but are struggling today include GE, Citicorp, Boeing, Hewlett-Packard, Motorola, and Merck. The rules are changing.

In the second decade of the twenty-first century, companies must go beyond Hedgehog concept. In addition to Collins' Hedgehog, companies in the Conceptual Age must consider "Six Senses" as Daniel Pink describes in *A Whole New Mind: Why Right-Brainers Will Rule the Future*. Pink argues that in the age of abundance and Asian competition, we need to replace engineering with design. Steve Jobs designed. Rajan Suri has argued for more than a decade that manufacturers in the United States and Europe can compete by rethinking short runs and providing unlimited choices.[9] At fairs, vendors design t-shirts on demand. Can inexpensive custom designed cars be next? While we may not be there yet, Rajan Suri and others have helped reinvigorate old industries by limiting work in process in short-run processes. Labor costs in many durable goods are less than 10 percent. We can compete.

Define Year 5 in Profitability and Market Share

Most small businesses see profit as that which at is left over at the end of the year. If they want more profit, they work harder, expand, and do more of what they have been doing. Successful companies picture ourselves in the future. What does our product and service look like? Who is buying it? What makes us different from our competitors? How can we improve our position? Do we redesign? Do we improve logistics or networks? What is my product or service going to look like? How much do we need to sell? Must we add or drop products or services to meet expectations? How much profit do we have to make to meet our financial goals? We fix our goals and build the business around them. We must be players, not victims.

Reverse Engineer Years 1 through 5

Most small businesses project forward. Successful companies plan backward from future goals. As we work backward, we expose weaknesses. If our current product or service mix cannot reasonably support the required growth, we find alternatives.

Focusing on Time, Purpose, Design, and Thinking Small Does Fit Together

Focus on time minimizes investments in infrastructure. Get finished goods out the door quickly and eliminate WIP. Think small. Do not overcommit to buildings, big machinery, or massive distribution networks. Broad purpose opens new product possibilities. If you choose a broad market and stay flexible, you can change as the world changes.

CHAPTER 3

Execution

Planning Starts Top Down

Shareholders and owners decide its purpose and provide corporate vision. Senior managers define the one-year mission with shareholders' approval. From there, it should be an iterative process. Employees must be involved with the *how*; we must get enterprise-wide input and buy-in.

With our core purpose, product and service definitions, and sense of size that we want in five years, we are ready to build our company. The Japanese called it *Hoshin Kanri*. A similar corporate tool was developed in the West called Balanced Score Card. As discussed in chapter 1, success is often opportunity crossing preparation. We need to prepare multiple corporate capabilities at once. By balanced action, I mean multiple, simultaneous action to avoid disruption.

> One defense contractor client had an extraordinary opportunity when their rainmaker won a game-changing bid. Unfortunately, we had no corporate alignment.
>
> **We must align all corporate functions simultaneously.** My client was used to winging it. They had no true estimating practices in place. Our rainmaker was a poor manager and had no backup. We had a poorly defined bonus system. For a year, we operated in chaos.

We won key bids but paid dearly for not having other functions well defined. We nearly lost our company.

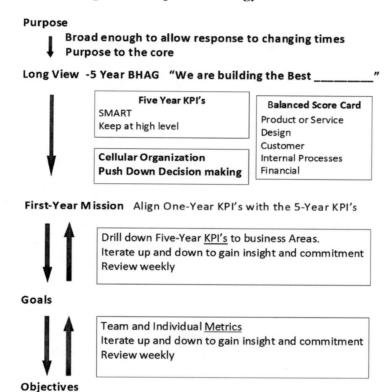

Figure 1 Corporate Strategy Has Order

Long View

Collins in *Built to Last* defined a term BHAG or *big hairy audacious goal.*[10] Think what can be, not what is. From the BHAG, comes vision; vision leads to "what is our five-year market share and dollar target." We make our vision clear. We develop *key performance indicators* (KPIs) that are SMART: specific, measurable, agreed-upon, realistic, and trackable. "In five years we will

1. take 50 percent of our market,
2. reduce set up or change over costs by 90 percent,

3. reduce lead times from three weeks to one day,
4. achieve $10,000,000 cash flow,
5. etc."

Drill Down to Year 1

It is hard to motivate people with a five-year goal. Ultimately, most employees respond at best to quarterly goals. We start with a one-year mission statement, again including market share and dollar targets. "In year one, we will

1. move from 5 percent market share to 10 percent,
2. reduce set up or change over costs by 50 percent,
3. reduce lead times from three weeks to four days,
4. achieve $3,000,000 annual cash flow,
5. etc."

We break it down further to quarterly and monthly targets.

Goals

Define key performance indicators or KPIs. At this stage we might hold kaizen events to match big leaps in efficiencies to close gaps between where we are today to where we need to be. We will discuss kaizen events in chapter 8. If possible, we might benchmark top companies in any given area.

Cellular Organizations

Flattening organizations came about because technology reduced the need for layers of management. Unfortunately, many companies continue to organize functionally. Many managers believe that only specialists can receive orders, others can only process orders, and only Joe can operate a lathe. We have a department for everything.

American managers underestimate workers and often get what they expect. Agility to win world competition demands cross-training, pushed-down scheduling and decision-making, and cellular operations. That requires trust and respect for our employees.

Team Metrics

When translating Taiichi Ohno's *Seven Waste to Americans*, Womack et al (2003), noted a cultural difference between Japanese management and American.[11] For Japan to rapidly modernize after WWII, companies were force to use its available talent. There were few engineers in Japan after the war. The militaristic Samurai society had to give way to building an inclusive society. The Japanese had a sense of community, which led companies to include all of their male talent. American corporate culture was top down. Management made decisions and rarely sought workers opinions. Womack noted an eighth waste for Americans, "waste of unused human talent." Not only did Americans lose input from the very people closest to work problems and consumption, they also lost the opportunity to motivate. The best companies excel in using *everyone*.

Once management adopts top-level goals, we align lower levels. Since our goals our stretched, we need every employee to improve. Improvement demands measures. We need metrics to monitor progress and hold focus. We incorporate as many leading metrics as we can. Monthly profits look back; productivity metrics portend the future. In addition, managers need to cede control of worker's metrics. Typically, low-level metrics are team metrics. Recognizing and rewarding teams, multiplies supervision. Peer pressure motivates. Metrics should be easy to measure, graph and understand. Table 1 illustrates detailed metrics.

Table 1   From Broad KPIs to Metrics

Metric	Function Measured	Target	Actual
Gross Profit as a % of sales	General management	44.80%	40.50%
Total G&A expense as a % of sales	General management	17.60%	19.20%
Cost of sales (selling expense) as a % of total sales	Sales	4.40%	4.30%
% of revenue forecast attainment	Sales	100%	90%
% of Product A Forecast (related to Market Share)	Sales	100%	90%
% of Product B Forecast (related to Market Share)	Sales	100%	90%
% of Product C Forecast (related to Market Share)	Sales	100%	90%
% of Product D Forecast (related to Market Share)	Sales	100%	90%
Avg time from receipt of order to order approval	Inside sales	30	120
Customer satisfaction Surveys, 1 low, 5 high	Inside Sales	4	3
Days AR outstanding	Finance & Admin	45	57.9
AP days outstanding	Finance & Admin	25	32
% turnover	HR	0	5
Production equipment up time	Production Eng	95%	85%
Service orders issued / % complete	Production Eng	95%	85%
Average Supplier lead time, days	Purchasing	10	1
Inventory Days	Purchasing	90	100
5S's grading and measurement	Production Mgr	100%	90%
Days without lost time accidents	Production Mgr	1000	1520
% scrap cost vs. cost of material produced	Production Mgr	1%	4%
Average Order to ship lead times in days	Scheduler	4	7
Schedule attainment rate (% on-time deliveries)	Scheduler	100%	98%
Overtime labor hours as a % of total labor hours	Scheduler	0%	10%
Finished Goods inventory offs per 100 pulls	Scheduler	0%	2%
# of finished parts / hour / station	Supervisors	25	100
% order complete	Supervisors	90%	90%
% rejects per 1000 elements produced	Supervisors	0%	5%
% product cured vs. theoretical yield	Supervisors	95%	85%
Raw materials inventory offs per 1000 pulls	Inventory Supervisor	1	50
Orders returned from customer	QA Supervisor	0%	0%
% scrap $ to cost of goods material	Inventory Supervisor	1%	4%

The extended table includes variances and frequency of reporting. We measure performance to metrics as a team and as an individual. Further, metrics tend to be leading indicators of the company's health. Incentive plans should focus on performance to metrics based on predetermined targets. We post and discussed metrics weekly. We chart trends.

Low-level metrics support higher-level ones and the KPIs. It is a top-down and bottoms-up process. The Japanese call this iterative process *Nemawashi*, literally translated as *catch ball*.

Metrics must directly support Year One KPIs and be easily understood, measured, and graphed. Table 1 is an abbreviated table of metrics from a client. These are dashboard metrics and should be as leading as possible. Further, the shop floor or office must clearly understand how the metric is measured and to what level to improve.

We measure daily and meet weekly. We communicate, communicate, and communicate more! Any employee that is unmoved by daily discussions of metrics should go. We must demand commitment to improvement.

Ultimately, we need to chart metrics to see trends. We have found control charts have enough statistical history that we can quickly see if improvement is real.

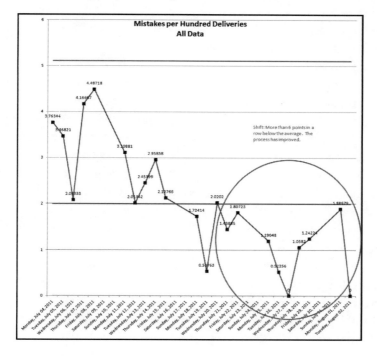

Figure 2   Example of a Control Chart

There are multiple sources available to explain control charts. Please consider *Improving Healthcare with Control Charts: Basic and Advanced SPC*

Methods and Case Studies by Raymond Carey and Larry Stake.[12] Most people think of control charts are used exclusively in manufacturing. I chose a reference and an example to show how broadly control charts can be used. The chart in figure 2 illustrates delivery mistakes. My Six Sigma friends would be horrified to see the scale: mistakes per hundred deliveries. We worked to get the mistake rate down to one mistake every two thousand deliveries. It is not Six Sigma levels, but a significant improvement nonetheless. Six Sigma is single digits errors per one million occurrences. Indeed, I have set up control charts for my golfing friends. Control charts need to evolve from shop floors and used more in business. Control charts have advantages over simple time series plots in that control charts have well-defined statistics to define when a change is statistically relevant. Employees do not need to understand the statistics to either plot data or understand its significance. Determining whether a process has changed is an easy visual read. Simple visual rules include a plotted point exceeds minimum or maximum lines, six or more points in a row are above or below the average, six points in sequence trend up or down, and as many as nine other rules. These are rules that indicate a significant change has occurred. We need a minimum of eighteen measurements to show an operation is in control. Being in control defines areas under the graph where 99.73 percent of all points fall. Other conditions define under control. Again, our Green Belt can set the control chart up; after that, we can train any one to read the visual clues. If a point falls outside this region, the condition that led to the outlier is likely significantly different from recent past operations. We use control charts to test improvement efforts or monitor routine operations. Banks, insurance companies or any industry should employ control charts.

Standardized data are more useful. As an example, each store may have different levels of business—we cannot compare mistakes per day for a large store to a smaller store. We can compare one store with another or this year versus last year with standardized data. That is, rather than charting mistakes per day, we use mistakes per hundred deliveries. Another example is inventory turnover, which is more relevant in comparison to other like companies than absolute dollar values. Your accounts receivables should change as you grow, but your days receivables may not. These are standardized data.

All employees need reinforcement on a frequent basis if you want to change. Metrics make progress or lack of progress clear. Discussing progress frequently keeps change in everyone's forethoughts. Celebrate significant improvements immediately. Talking about the past year at your Christmas party is too late.

CHAPTER 4

Mass versus Short-Run Responsive Production and Services

Daniel Pink talks about how the West must move beyond the Information Age and design products and services. He asserts we are in the age of abundance where winners lead by designing products that stimulate demand. Many mass producers or services have moved offshore. Consequently, the West needs to move to flexible short-run capabilities. Table 2 compares mass production to short-run or boutique production and services.

The vast majority of the US Fortune 500 companies having a significant engineering component have embraced Lean Six Sigma. Unfortunately, small to medium businesses have not. Since small to midsize companies tend to operate short runs, it is important to understand how to apply Lean Six Sigma. Table 2 illustrates the differences in implementing Lean Six Sigma in mass production versus short runs. The list of similarities is greatly abbreviated. While Dr. Suri makes a point of how Lean Six Sigma is less applicable to short-run applications, I have found many of the practices in quick response manufacturing more a question of focus rather than a separate practice. Nonetheless, Dr. Suri has made a significant contribution in advancing manufacturing technology.

Table 2 Mass Production vs. Short-Run Production

Mass Production & Services	Short-Run Production and Services
How They Differ in Focus	
Same item reproduced more than 5,000	One of a kind up to 5,000 reproductions
Use statistical controls–Six Sigma. Use Takt time to optimize cellular flow. Focus on efficiencies	Use Quick Response Manufacturing and Uses statistical controls but less well Focuses on causes for delay and
Examples: Reviewing insurance claims, making bottles or toys, call centers.	Examples: machine shops, teaching, auto repair service.
High standardization.	Low standardization.
Focuses on overall equipment effectiveness.	Focuses on uninterrupted production or service in addition to eight wastes.
Strives for high percent capacity utilization.	Should strive to maintain 85 percent or less capacity utilization.
Biggest delays are caused by eight wastes.	Biggest delays are caused by waiting between operations, scheduling chaos,
Amenable to Kanban and "pull" scheduling and control of inventory.	Amenable to POLCA or control by coupling unit capacity availabilities and "pull".
How They Are Alike	
Reduction in work-in-progress reduces eight waste, improves quality and reduces shop foot print.	Reduction in work-in-progress reduces eight waste, improves quality and reduces shop foot print.
Focus on cycle time improves costs and quality.	Focus on cycle time improves costs and quality.
Cross-training workers to perform multiple tasks is preferable to specializing.	Cross-training workers to perform multiple tasks is preferable to specializing.
Low work-in-progress is best practice.	Small batches or Single-piece flow and elimination of work-in progress is best.
Control Charts are best improvement tools.	Control Charts are best improvement tools.
Maintaining 5S's across the enterprise is critical.	Maintaining 5S's across the enterprise is critical.
Cellular flow is best in production and across the organization (maximize teams and matrix organization is best).	Cellular flow is best in production and across the organization (maximize teams and matrix organization is best).

Since the industrial revolution, managers tended to believe the following things:

- Many jobs require specialized training, and consequently, organize along specialized functions.
- As a corollary, we need to separate large equipment to perform specialized tasks.
- We need to operate with large batches to reduce the per-unit costs for setting up equipment or changing a service process.
- Managers should be rewarded for keeping production costs low. Because traditional accounting includes absorbed labor in inventories, running excess inventory is encouraged.
- If something goes wrong, blame the operator.

I have been amazed how managers are blind to waste. Having to constantly move work-in-process or weave around stacks of inventory seems a small price to pay for having the best operator doing all the trim work. If we can convince our supervisors to try single-piece flow and compare the output to their old batch process, we can usually show the waste. Unfortunately, it is often difficult to set up a valid single piece runs. Often large equipment is often difficult to move temporarily.

I have found that taking a familiar task, such as stuffing envelopes for mailing, a good teaching opportunity. To teach virtues of single-piece flow, I prepare twelve sets of ten envelops with windows, ten sheets of paper, ten pencils, and ten stamps. I bring the production group to the company break room and have two teams of six sit across from each other. Each person has the sets of envelops, paper, pencils, and stamps on the table in front of them. I tell the Lean Team to do the following:

1. Place an X on the paper where the folded paper would have the mark show up in the window.
2. Then fold the paper in thirds to fit in the envelop.
3. Stuff the envelop.
4. Check the window to if the X appears.
5. Put a Y where the return address would be.
6. Put a stamp on it.
7. Finally place the envelop in a central stack to be mailed.

Batch team completes the individual tasks with all ten letters before moving to the next task. That is, they were to replicate their real-life batch operation; they built WIP between all seven steps.

Every time I have tried this, the Lean team wins. Often, I find one batch player will misplace the *X*'s in the windows. When he does, he repeats the mistake with several letters. He does not recognize his mistake until he begins stuffing letters. I ask if this occurs in their regular work. I usually get a yes.

They can see how having to stack the work-in-progress doubles workspace required.

I use this familiar task because it would be too difficult to demonstrate batch versus single-piece flow without moving large monuments. I use at least six people on a team because there is always a ringer that can stuff envelops quickly on the batch side. Further, I expect at least one person on the batch side to reproduce *X*'s that do not fit into the window.

While cross-training workers to perform multiple tasks is preferable to developing specialists, we do need to learn from the most proficient and effective workers. As part of cross-training, we should study, benchmark, and transfer skills from those showing the most proficiency.

In addition to believing specialists can do a better job, managers are quick to blame workers for mistakes. Ironically, when an employee makes a mistake, it is because the process is set up for failure. If the process is not error proofed, whose fault is that? Japanese call making a process error proof, *Poka-Yoke*.

Traditional accounting encourages overproduction and consumes cash. I once ran a synthetic lubricants base oil business for Chevron Chemicals. Our sales varied little month to month. We had enough capacity to generate a calendar quarter's inventory in one month. When we overproduced inventory in one month, excess inventory absorbed labor costs and was put on the balance sheet. The company rewarded my division. For the next two nonproducing months, balance sheet inventory released labor, and now we were slackers. Sales or prices never budged. Plant managers take advantage of faux accounting by building inventory at the end of the year. On paper production cost dropped. They got their bonuses. No one questioned cash hidden in inventory. Throughput accounting eliminates this shell game. In throughput accounting, production costs consider only material costs.

CHAPTER 5

Understand the Dynamics of Improvement: Part 1

Variation Is the Enemy

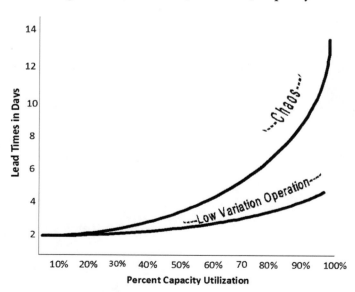

Figure 3 Lead Times, Variation, Capacity

The company operating in chaos in figure 3 had become accustomed to seven—to ten-day lead times. With all this time, they constantly interrupt production flow as WIP shifts between groups and priorities change. My client would interrupt production when his best customers called. Chaos feeds on itself, pushing delivery dates further behind. My client told me that when they started and had few customers, they could deliver product in twenty-four hours.

After changing their culture as described over the next few pages, my client brings his operations under control. Yes, lead times increase when we get busier but at a shallower pace. Operating with low variation, my client could promise four-day deliveries.

While we were studying operations, I noticed that order takers were constantly in the production area. They were expediting rush orders. A previous consultant suggested we hire an expeditor. Does anyone reading this book believe we can ever justify an expeditor? Read on.

Customers feel variation more than averages. Do you remember your average wait in a doctor's office or the one time you waited two hours? Customers can adjust to expected wait times; variation is the enemy.

Single-Piece Flow Increases Throughput and Reduces Footprints

We demonstrate how single-piece flow is faster than batching by stuffing, sealing, and marking envelops. As an added complication, I compared the two systems to crowd control through an amusement park. My analogy is with two equally popular rides that take four people on a ride for five minutes. *Lean Mountain* gives riders a clock with the exact time they can board the ride. See figure 4. They only have room for four people in a queue so four people show up a few minutes before the ride. *Batch Mountain* has unlimited queuing lines through mazes but lets people get in line whenever

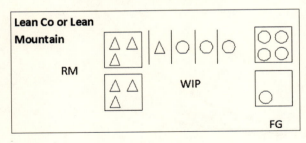

Figure 4 Lean Company

Figure 5 Batch Company

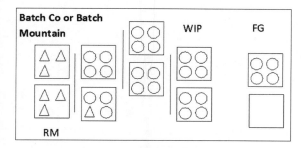

they want. See figure 5. *Lean Mountain* requires less than ten minutes to complete rides once they get in their queue. *Batch Mountain* has a two-hour wait on average. The riders in the unlimited queue try to time their entry according to the time of day. Because the lines vary all day and they were trying to come at a perfect time, they often missed their window and their wait-time spilled over to the next day.

In real-life operation, we start a new batch while we are completing the old. We fill all work in progress, WIP, before we can generate finished product. In batch operations, that can take hours or days. Since single-piece-flow operations have limited WIP, we start making new product almost immediately.

Little's law demonstrates how reducing work in process reduces lead-time:

$$Lead\ Time = \frac{Amount\ of\ Work\text{-}in\text{-}Progress}{Average\ Completion\ Rate}$$

That is *lead times* are proportional to the amount of *work in progress* we have on the shop floor or in any service. Little's law is the mathematical explanation of why it takes longer to move through the lines in Batch Co than in Lean Co.

If you manufacture one-of-a-kind products, single-piece flow means we start and finish one project at a time. I asked a large metal pole barn builder what it was like in their busy season. He said that they fill his entire one hundred thousand square-foot warehouse. He was planning to double space to accommodate growth. He even was training someone whose sole function was to move work in process from place to place. To optimize his equipment that shapes and cuts metal panels for buildings, he would run all projects requiring gray panels of a certain width. Then he would use the blue coils of steel, then brown, and so forth. Consequently, the builder would amass building units of several pallets of wood studs, metal panels, and supplies for multiple barns. Clearly, he saved changeover costs. What the builder failed to see was the multiple times he had to move the lots to get to raw materials or the costs for panels damaged in the moves. Most importantly, he did not see the creep in delivery delays. In emergencies, the builder could generate the materials for a building in twenty-four to forty-eight hours. In their busy seasons, they told customers it would take four to six weeks. We focused on minimizing work in progress and getting building units out the door before starting a new project. Manufacturing took one-fourth of the space. By managing customer expectations, he could still optimize by running similar colored steel coils. Because he could get units out the door much quicker, he still managed to meet customer expectations. He did not lose customers by overpromising and interrupting production when his biggest customer called. Again, the obvious is often wrong.

Common sense led my client, who built limousine body panels and windows, to stock twenty to thirty panels each for year models of Lincolns, Cadillacs, Hummers, and Mercedeses. He was proud that he built the inventory over fifteen years and could respond to customers quickly. I asked how much money had he invested in inventory? What did that large warehouse cost him? Most importantly, how much of his inventory was obsolete? Even though he had taken little money out of the company in his fifteen years, he still had little cash flow despite the goldmine for which he was so proud. We spent the bulk of my time learning how to exchange dies in minutes (SMED). That is, how to reduce set-up time. We prebuilt jigs and guides. We used three people to change over equipment instead of one. We stored sheets of metal and glass rather than finished parts. We revamped the glass shaping equipment. To pay for retraining, I convinced the owner to sell his treasured inventory even at a paper loss. While he cannot supply limousine panels out of inventory, he does have a twenty-four-hour delivery policy, and he ships nationwide because his costs have come down.

The plastic injection mold industry is a great example of the evolution of single-minute exchange of dies (SMED). When I traveled across the United States in 1980 renting equipment to test new polyethylene resins, a typical injection mold took a half an hour or more to exchange. This drove companies to make excess plastic parts for possible future orders. The dies were bolted with as many as six bolts. Using racing cars as their example, one company moved to a single-bolt system. Today, some molds are attached electromagnetically and pop off in a second.

I found multiple other examples. A wooden pallet maker filled his plant with excess pallets because it takes too long to adjust his equipment for different dimensions. He told me his constraint was forklifts. He could only operate two because of all the WIP and finished goods took up too much space. His operator would run as many pallets as he thought he could sell in six months. He told me it takes his operator two hours to realign his automated nailer. We designed preset jigs for each pallet dimension and used four people instead of one to realign his equipment. Change over went from two hours to less than ten minutes. He uses one-fourth of the warehouse space and has more than doubles his productivity. He no longer moves WIP and finished goods multiple times. Forklifts were no longer the constraint. Offices use more templates to rapidly move from job to job. I can save my clients substantial consulting costs by using templates. Households download legal templates for family business. Yes, it takes time and creativity to create templates, or make your home screen on your computer more user friendly or redesigning your equipment. Applying a few thoughtful hours developing templates saves thousands of wasted hours. When I was a research chemist, we would say, "One day in the library was worth a week in the lab." Study any process you use repeatedly and find a way to cut time between jobs.

Biggest Opportunity to Reduce Lead Times Is to Reduce White Space[13]

Dr. Suri divides time from receiving an order to delivering a product or services into touch time and white space. Touch times are segments that move the process forward. In Lean, it is called value add time. This might include the time to take an order, entering an order, scheduling production, and steps in fabrication and assembly, packaging and shipping. Suri defines white space as "wait time or time where work in progress sits in a queue." Most companies are shocked that white space is 90 percent of lead time.

Table 3 Typical Steps in a Manufacturing Procss

1. Order received	12. Tray ready for production	23. Mnfg C
2. Entered into computer	13. Pick up	24. WIP
3. Tray for cross check	14. Scheduling	25. Mnfg D
4. Cross check	15. Kitting inventory	26. WIP
5. Return from cross check	16. Traveler in tray for supervisor	27. Move
6. Tray for return	17. Floor space prepared	28. WIP
7. Corrections in computer	18. Supervisor schedules	29. Pack
8. Tray for orders ready	19. Mnfg A	30. Finished Goods
9. Engineer picks up	20. WIP	31. Move
10. Attach traveler	21. Mnfg B	32. Finished Goods Staged
11. Second engineer approves	22. WIP	33. Ship

I have had an opportunity to help manufacturers that had over the years allowed their lead time slip from days to weeks. As an example, one company saw its lead time slip from four days to eight. We tracked every step in their process. See table 3.

White space showed up between each of the thirty-three steps in Table 3. In fact, more than 95 percent of the time tracked was white space. Ironically, most engineers focus on improving times for the 5 percent touch time. The biggest problem was that there was no person or team driving a product through the system. Our first step was to assign responsibility and accountability to a person or team for as many steps as possible. We cross-train to allow one team to follow to completion. Our goal was to eliminate white space by not allowing orders or WIP to sit between activities.

We made steps 1 through 14 electronic. We provided screening rules for the program to sort which orders required a second engineering review. After tracking, we found the second engineer only had to review two percent of the production orders. Before, our second engineer was sorting through every order. We eliminated steps 20, 22, 24, 26, 28, and 30. We immediately reduced lead times from a median of eight days to four.

When companies run in chaos, lead times creep longer. Where they once could generate most equipment in twenty-four hours, they were so busy now that their delivery stretched to a median of eight days. In one case, we had to move work in process over one hundred yards between two operations. Work piled up between functions, and there was no single person or team to push work to shipment. Not only did lead times suffer, the company was constantly building warehouse and manufacturing space. While they were in a very profitable market, inefficiencies and costs for space were beginning to limit their growth and eat away at profits.

Cellular Operations

Cellular operations refer to one team completing production from start to finish using single-piece flow. The opposite of cellular operations is functional operations. Functional operations pass batches from one department to another with no single identifiable person or group responsible. Companies go to functional systems to take advantage of specialists. Almost every company that has switched to cellular organizations reports dramatic increases in productivity. This is true for manufacturing and services. People can be cross-trained, and the potential loss in having specialists is more than offset by the efficiency.

Figure 6 Cellular Manufacturing

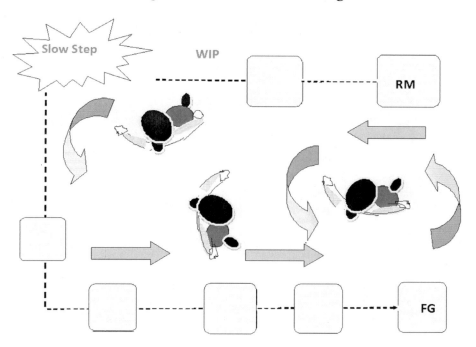

Figure 6 shows the characteristics of cellular operations on the shop floor. RM is raw materials; FG is finished goods. One or more people complete the constraining step (slow step). For the fast steps, one person can complete multiple operations.

The most efficient cellular operation is U shaped or a horseshoe. By folding back operations, one operator can handle multiple tasks across the line. This enables load leveling.

Cellular offices have a single person take the order, having the resources to approve engineering and working with his or her customer and production team on project scheduling. We can accomplish this electronically.

As an aside, if you had the operation in figure 6, which step would you work on to increase throughput? Where does WIP pile up?

Focus on Dramatically Reducing Lead Times and Not On-Time Deliveries

The *obvious* is often wrong in short-run or job shop manufacturing. If you focus on increasing on-time deliveries, overall on-time deliveries actually get worse over time. Here is a partial list of the reasons why.

1. Focusing on on-time deliveries often requires us to break into current production runs to expedite orders. Yes, we expedite that one order, but it creates *chaos* everywhere else. WIP piles up. Other schedules must adjust. We expedite more orders. I often see the order taker leave her desk to push the order through production. We often have to get a sales person involved to explain late deliveries. We lose business. Most of these costs are hidden.
2. *Chaos* is another word for operation variability. Variability has a dramatic impact on lead times when we push capacity. Lead time is the time it takes to complete a job and ship.
3. Focusing on on-time delivery causes supervisors along the chain to pad their quoted times, if they are measured on on-time completion.
4. Supervisors do jobs ahead of time to fill slow time. This increases WIP, not only ties up resources, it also causes excess movement of inventory, exposes product to damage and clogs production lanes. The job to fill dead time may conflict with an unexpected urgent order coming in. It would be better to use idle time to cross-train, work on continuous improvement, discuss reducing set-up time, or just send people home.

Conversely, Focus on Lead Times to Dramatically Improve Overall Percent of On-time Deliveries

Professor Suri, in *It's About Time: The Competitive Advantage of Quick Response Manufacturing*, gives example of improvements after focusing on reducing lead times.[14] Ninety percent reductions in lead times have led to improvements in percent of on-time deliveries from as low as 20 to 95 percent. These were all job shops that made large varieties of specialized parts in low volume. Professor Suri created the Quick Response Manufacturing (QRM) department at the University of Wisconsin in 1988. Hundreds of job shops around the United States and Europe use his techniques to stay competitive with China and India. Quick response manufacturing is compatible with and similar to Lean. In companies that Suri installed QRM, inventories were reduced significantly and responsiveness to customers increased. When times for manufacturing critical paths were reduced from 57 to 94 percent, production costs dropped 13-20 percent and rework or rejects dropped by a factor of ten.

Bottom line: Reduced lead times would allow companies to respond to customers quicker with less chaos.

Focus on Keeping People and Equipment Busy Leads to Wrong Decisions

I had an opportunity to improve a large automotive maintenance shop. The repair shop had lost two of five master mechanics and could not find a replacement. Fortunately, it was February, a slow month in the repair business. They had twelve bays and used several apprentices. I noticed that the $40 per hour master mechanics often left their bays to find tools and look for parts and materials. We hired $10 per runner and did the 5Ss improvement. See chapter 9. We took doors off cabinets so we could visually see if we were low on filters, rags, etc. (The 5Ss allowed for a major improvement in productivity.) We threw out old equipment and organized bays with every tool or all supply they use daily. We shadowed their toolboxes to ensure mechanics replaced tools in their exact position. By April, their busy season, they produced twice the business and never had to rehire two master mechanics.

I called in June. The owner said they were falling behind. I returned to the repair shop. I noticed the $10 per hour runner were mowing their lawn and running errands for the owner. I asked the owner why the runners had left their posts. The owner said that he noticed there were times where the runners were standing around idle. Therefore, he found other work for them to do. Because of the compulsion to keep everyone busy, he diverted the runners from their reasons for existence: to keep the master mechanics in the bays repairing cars. They were losing thousands of dollars in order to keep a ten dollar an hour runner busy. Smart? To be competitive, short-run operations have to keep capacity below 80 percent.

Remember, successful job shops run at less than 80 percent capacity on average. The irony is that by running at 80 percent capacity on average, we serviced more cars and made more money. As you near capacity, you start making more mistakes—you miss customer deliveries. Chaos grows exponentially. You use more inventories to cover. Large inventories take up valuable space and require multiple wasted moves. Managers call emergency meetings. We overuse air or rush freight. We force overtime. We shortcut safety and standard procedures. We increase rework and scrap.

Do Not Misplace Compassion

On a larger scale, keeping a community alive by sacrificing opportunity serves no one. *The Wall Street Journal* had a headline on January 12, 2012 by Forbes publisher Rich Karlgaard, "Kodak Didn't Kill Rochester. It Was the Other Way Around: The film pioneer invented the digital camera but couldn't escape the intellectual limitations of geography." Mr. Karlgaard argued that because Kodak had such a large footprint in Rochester, it failed to capitalize on changing technology. Kodak underserved Rochester by keeping alive technology that was being displaced. In the end, false compassion led to even greater devastation. Yes, as human beings we should be compassionate. On the other hand, I never understood how owners could focus on the plight of one or a few individuals, while the jobs of hundreds or thousands are threatened. I have told an owner to pay his sister-in-law a salary for not working, if the sister-in-law was killing the company. An owner or manager's first responsibility is the health of the company. Small sacrifices for the sake of compassions are appropriate. Clearly, giving extended time off for family matters not only shows compassion, but it also returns dividends to the company in the end. Failure to respond to life threats is stupid.

CHAPTER 6

Understand the Dynamics of Improvement: Part 2

Focusing on Efficiency for Short-Run Operations is Counterproductive

Optimizing efficiencies for individual operations in job shops actually makes the enterprise's costs worse. Often, we find adding people or equipment speeds up throughput, which has a dramatically positive impact on the enterprise. Unfortunately, standard accounting systems will only show increased production labor and depreciation. Standard accounting does not relate dramatically reduced lead times, increased throughput, reduced expediting chaos and our competitive advantage to labor, and equipment costs. Activity based accounting shows profitability gains far out paces the increase in labor or equipment costs.

Rather than focusing on efficiencies, focus on lead times. Track causes for delays. An engine machine shop filled out Table 4. On Fridays, we would look at what are the most frequent causes of delays and then look for root causes.

Table 4 Check List to Track Work Flow Delays

Stoppage	1	2	3	4	5	6	7	8	9	10	Total	Reason
Customer												
Vendor												
Vacation												
Schedule Screw Up												
Machine Breakdown												
Rework												
Poor Internal Communication												
Hot Job or Emergencies												
Answer Phones												
Find Job												
Looking for Parts												
Walking Between Stations												
Rating												
Less than 1 hour	Action for Next											
1-4 hours	1											
4-8 hours	2											
1-2 days	3											
More than 2 days	4											

Theory of constraints (TOC) argues that there can be only one constraint at a time. TOC asks, "Why improve efficiencies around non-constrained resources only to increase WIP in front of the constraint?" That is one area where I found theory of constraints in conflict with Lean. Lean seeks to load level. That is, we match each individual task to Takt time. The implication, I found, was that we size each piece of equipment to keep the rhythm of throughput. In TOC, we argue that we should maintain excess equipment capacity upstream of the constraint. TOC recognizes that should the non-constrained resource have any hic up and failed to feed the constraint, through put suffers. I have noted that when Lean proponents teach TOC, they frequently ignore TOC's tenant that there can be only one constraint. I favor TOC's perspective.

As an aside, while Goldratt greatly added to our body of knowledge, engineers used the tenets of TOC long before Goldratt's, *The Goal*.[16] See the following section for a discussion of TOC. We applied linear programming to design large petrochemical plants. That is, we identified the most expensive piece of equipment and used it to set the capacity of the plant. We then designed less expensive equipment with excess capacity to ensure we never starved the constraint. Goldratt applied this engineering concept across the enterprise.

Look to Operations to Increase Capacity before Spending Money

Most companies operate near capacity. Consequently, we operate in chaos as we reach our capacity by rushing things. We increase lead times and other operating costs. Look at figure 3. The closer we get to capacity, the longer lead times.

Often we can reduce capacity utilization without capital. We should consider the following:

1. Optimizing product mix in sales to focus on products best suited to our operations.
2. Redesigning products to consolidate parts and minimize complexity.
3. Scheduling like-specification products to reduce equipment changeovers.
4. Reducing set-up times. This not only impacts operation times but it also reduces the temptation to run large batches.
5. Expanding shifts.
6. Adding people. Use idle time to cross-train.
7. Finding the one bottleneck and subordinate all operations to maximize through put at that one bottleneck.
8. Using less-efficient equipment to support a bottleneck. Add people to reduce the bottleneck.
9. Eliminating defects and reruns.
10. Eliminating production interruptions.
11. Reducing amounts we make to stock.
12. Reducing employee absenteeism.
13. Performing preventive maintenance to improve equipment up-time.

Theory of Constraints

Points 7 and 8 in the list above are major tenants of theory of constraint (TOC). Eliyahu Goldratt's *The Goal* was a seminal publication describing how throughput is always limited by a single bottleneck.[15] When we find the bottleneck, he offers step-by-step solutions to remove it. Once removed, a new bottleneck surfaces. Goldratt's prescription is

> **Table 5 Prescription from the Theory of Constraints**
>
> 1. Identify the constraint—the resource that limits throughput: . . . the critical chain, the piece of equipment, the service, etc.
> 2. Exploit it—get everything you can from it (the constraint). Never allow the constraint to be idle.
> 3. Subordinate all other actions to it—do not use the constrained resource if you can use another resource, even if it looks less efficient to do so. Improving the non-constrained resource is pointless.
> 4. Elevate it—find ways to increase its capacity.
> 5. Repeat the cycle—look for the next constraint.

Most people apply theory of constraints to manufacturing. I found a plumber that had to overcome his restraints.

Joe the Plumber and TOC

Joe has owned a plumbing shop for ten years. He earns about $50,000 per year, but needs more as his kids start to go to college. He has three employees who do most of the work. Joe loves to get his hands dirty and is the site manager. Joe also sells, answers the phone, estimates jobs, negotiates, buys materials, does the bookkeeping, and manages people during his eighty-hour week. As the only plumbing company in Small Town, USA, he has more business than he can handle. His competition comes from Big City, USA, about 40 miles away. How can Joe get more money? Figure 7 illustrates Joe's predicament. Joe needs to put more money through the "work-flow pipe" so he can send his kids through college. Joe believes he could generate at least $100,000 more business if he added a plumber. Because Joe does many of the jobs in his business, there are no bulges in the work-flow pipe. That is, it is difficult to identify the constraint because Joe covers several bases well enough to generate $50,000 in profits from $400,000 of current business. The constraint would appear as a narrow spot in the work-flow pipe.

Figure 7 Joe's Business Flow with $400,000 in Sales

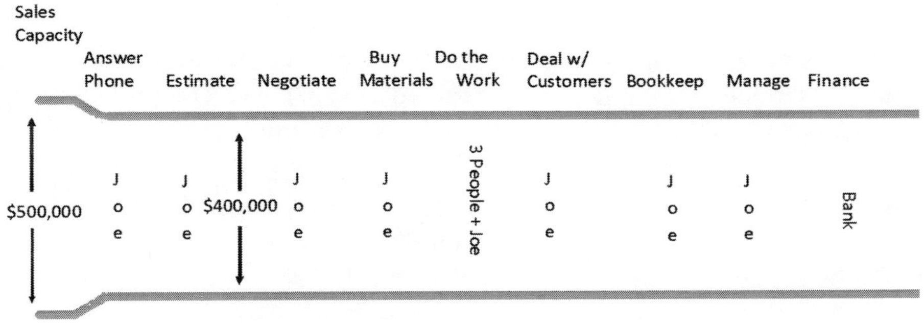

[Figure 7 diagram showing Joe's business flow pipeline with stages: Answer Phone, Estimate, Negotiate, Buy Materials, Do the Work (3 People + Joe), Deal w/ Customers, Bookkeep, Manage, Finance. Sales Capacity $500,000, with $400,000 marked at Negotiate stage.]

Joe's First Attempt Failed

Joe thinks he needs to add a plumber. In TOC terms, Joe thought his constraint was not enough plumbers. See figure 8. As soon as Joe added a new apprentice, the company's costs go up; Joe must take time to manage his new apprentice. Since Joe cannot increase the number of hours in a week, he will have to reduce time dealing with customers or other vital work. Operating capital becomes negative and the company will not be able to finance jobs at $400,000 rate. Joe goes back to old system.

In the work-flow pipe analogy, while Joe did increase the plumber capacity, rather than expanding the pipe, he created a bulge in a narrower chamber.

Figure 8 Joe Constraint Identifies the Wrong Constraint

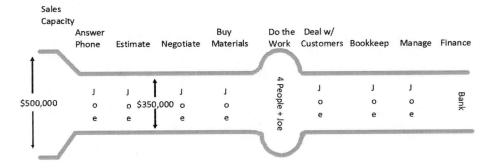

Joe the Plumber's TOC Solution:
Increase Joe's Capacity to Perform the Other Duties.

The fact that Joe does many jobs hides his constraint. Indeed, the constraint is Joe. In fact, Joe's next move was to hire office help. Joe focused on plumbing until he could build more sales. When Joe was administratively capable of handing more work, he hired a fourth plumber and concentrated on getting new business and training the new plumber. When he made more money, he financed an expansion. Joe had the money to pay for a local college. Sales became the new constraint. See figure 9.

Figure 9 Joe the Plumber Uses Theory of Constraint

Sales Capacity	Answer Phone	Estimate	Negotiate	Buy Materials	Do the Work	Deal w/ Customers	Bookkeep	Manage	Finance
$500,000	New Office Help	Joe $600,000	Joe	New Office Help	4 People + Joe	Joe	New Office Help	Joe Trains Site Manager	Bank

New throughput $500,000

Put Joe's situation in TOC's context.

1. Identify the constraint—Joe cannot work more than eighty hours a week
2. Exploit it—get everything you can from it. Teach Joe how to manage. Train one of the plumbers to be a site supervisor.
3. Subordinate all other actions to it—do not let Joe do hands-on plumbing, even if he is the only master plumber in the company.
4. Elevate it—find ways to increase its capacity. Bring in office help. Grow. Then bring in an apprentice plumber.

5. Repeat the cycle—look for the next constraint. Sales become the next constraint. By increasing his profile locally, Joe should be able to displace his remote competition.

Take Multiple Buffers Away from Projects

While we have argued for single-piece flow and cellular operations, sometimes it is best to sublet operations. Subletting operations forces us back to functions. Rather than having a single team driving production, we send out or bring in specialists. We can learn from construction companies how to deal with subcontractors. Developing property requires multiple subcontractors. Laws generally prevent cross-training trades. Consequently, large jobs can take a year to construct and often depend on multiple trades from practicing or designing architecture, excavating, laying the foundation, pouring cement, framing, plumbing, dry-walling, painting, and doing the interior work. In designing and building large apartment complexes, we applied critical chain management to speed up construction and reduce costs. Critical chain project management was first described by Dr. Eliyahu M. Goldratt.[16]

Let me go through a simplified version of critical chain project management. Again, the common wisdom is often wrong. How many times have you heard project managers proclaim, "We finished on time and on budget". Do we pop the champagne?

Even if every task finishes on time and on budget, should we celebrate. The simple nature of project tasks is that there is always variability. Doing a similar task may take ten days one time, but because the unexpected occurs, it takes fifteen days the next time. Ask any construction supervisor about the weather.

If you are completing all tasks on time, you are missing opportunities to improve. Think about it. Subcontractors and managers often are rewarded for finishing on time and on budget. Frequently we impose liquidated damages if they do not. How do they avoid liquidated damages? most often by adding buffers. Suppose we had five subcontractors and each one added their own buffer. It is obvious. Now suppose you tell each subcontractor that he or she has half the time that he or she had quoted. What would happen? Most would finish in much less time than their original quote. A few may take longer because of weather or scheduling an inspector. The net result is that the complex construction project completes as much as 40 percent quicker and nearly 40 percent less labor costs. Actual critical chain project management adds a single buffer on critical sub-paths rather than allowing each subcontractor to add his or her own. Accounting for human behavior has been a game changer in many project-oriented businesses; any business that has to subcontract or uses Microsoft Project™ can apply these concepts.

As an aside, can you see where critical chain project management (CCPM) is a subset of TOC? Both anticipate variation in times to complete tasks. Rather than trying to make operation finish on a preset time, each accommodates variation by buffering only the constraint. Plants provide excess capacity up stream of its constraint. Maintaining excess capacity upstream increases costs at the task level but reduces costs at the enterprise level. In TOC, we do not try to optimize individual tasks efficiencies. CCPM does not try to smooth capacity by buffering individual tasks but adds buffers at the end. We optimize efficiencies of the entire process, not individual tasks. We started the book discussing time as a competitive weapon. TOC and CCPM are all about reducing lead times.

Don't Multitask

How many times have you heard people claim they are great multitaskers? Many people confuse activity for productivity. Let us explore the downside of multitasking:

1. Impact on pending projects
2. Need to reorient between tasks
3. Clutter causing wasted movement
4. Loss of insight
5. Opportunity loss
6. Little's law

1. Impact on pending projects

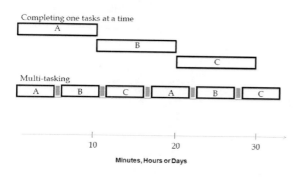

Figure 10 Multitasking: Reorientation Between Tasks

Suppose that in order to complete a project, we had to complete task A, then B, and so forth. While it seems trivial, if you have to halt your project to do another task, the project will minimally suffer from the time away. In the trivial case in figure 10, the project requiring steps A, B, C, and D is only delayed by the time of interruption.

2. Need to reorient or remobilize between tasks

The more complex your task or more materials that have to be remobilized, the longer completion of the original project will be. See figure 11. If a customer halts a project, many contractors charge a remobilization fee to restart. Even office work takes time to reorient when returning to a task.

3. Clutter causing wasted movement

To the extent the current task has to be moved or stored, we waste time. On the factory floor, it could mean extra forklift runs. Extra storage and movement of work in process is a waste. We build bigger warehouses, and time spirals out of control. In the office, either we file the unfinished task or we hide it under piles of paper.

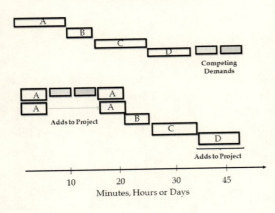

Figure 11 Multitasking: Impact on Pending Projects

4. Loss of insight

My best ideas have come during the middle of the night. Often breakthrough ideas come with an assist from the right brain. See chapter 12. We spend most the day thinking logically. Left-brain thinking is absolutely required to make incremental improvement. The overused term "out of the box" thinking often comes when we suspend reality—dream think. Edison used to take thirty-minute naps where he claimed to draw inspiration. If we are working on multiple projects, we lose focus. I often think of solutions at night or even at the water fountain. It is those times that my right brain assists the left. We see the whole; we may see an illogical juxtaposition. There is some benefit from saying, "Let me go home and sleep on it." We do not want to lose that wonderful assist by having our mind multitasking.

5. Opportunity loss

Let us say we have four projects to complete using all available resources. You decide to start all four projects at the same time and expect to finish in four weeks by multitasking. Even if we could avoid all the pitfalls discussed above, it would take four weeks to complete four tasks. Even though it may take the same time to complete all four projects, we lose the opportunity to please three customers in less than four weeks. Now, rather than dividing our resources to do all tasks concurrently, we put all resources to finish one project per week. I find many companies feel obligated to jump when their best customers or boss barks jump. To avoid multitasking, they must tell their boss or three of their best customers that they cannot start the project this week. That sounds trivial, but it is a real problem. This case is similar to short-run shops wanting to break into runs because our best customer calls. Yes, it may give one customer satisfaction; it delays all others.

Remember the lesson of having four people help change railings for an automatic nailer? They changed pallet dimensions under ten minutes rather than having one person take two hours. The company no longer had to make excess pallets to minimize per pallet change over costs. Now they serviced all customers quicker. Repair shops should put as many people as required on a job to get it out the door.

6. Little's law

I have mentioned Little's law before. It has value in the context of multitasking.

$$Lead\ Time = \frac{Amount\ of\ Work\text{-}in\text{-}Progress}{Average\ Completion\ Rate}$$

That is, the more we have unfinished, the longer it takes to complete everything.

CHAPTER 7

Reset Operations

To change from a functional job shop to a cellular operation, we need to reset operations. The two biggest issues are assigning a single person or team the responsibility to move product through all steps thus eliminating white space and separate responsibilities for on-time deliveries and reducing cycle time.

Scheduler's Responsibility and Authority

As we discussed in chapter 5, focusing on on-time delivery becomes counterproductive. On the other hand, on-time delivery is critical to winning and maintaining customers. So, how do we bridge the gap? We can assign the scheduler with the following responsibilities. He or she

1. is solely responsible for shipping product on or before agreed ship date,
2. assigns jobs to meet customers' demands,
3. ensures all parts and subassemblies are available to start job, including kitting "just-in-time" where appropriate;
4. controls ship date by controlling the assignment date and having the authority to authorize overtime, and
5. moves emergency orders to the top of the list.

Rationale

The scheduler must have a reasonable estimate of times required to run jobs. Once a job is scheduled, it runs uninterrupted. After he or she schedules the job, the scheduler's only control over hitting a promised ship date is his or her ability to authorize overtime.

Metric: Percent On-Time Deliveries

Manufacturing Team's Responsibility and Authority

1. Supervisors assign teams to complete jobs from gathering parts and subassemblies to delivering packaged finished goods to the loading dock.
2. The team's sole target is to manufacture products to beat standards for the cycle times for that particular product. That is, the team focuses on speed of delivery.

Rationale

Once a product is assigned to a team, manufacturing's only goal should be to deliver 100 percent acceptable quality product in the shortest possible time. That means the team must have total control of every step of manufacturing, from gathering parts to manufacturing to packaging to delivery. To the extent it makes sense, the scheduler can kit parts to ensure everything is available.

The manufacturing team should *not* consider any scheduled date since they are producing products as quickly as they can. If delivery is a problem, the scheduler should authorize overtime. At no time should a production line be interrupted. The goal is to minimize work in progress and wait times. Teams should track causes for delays and make continual improvements.

Metric: Number of units produced per unit time. As part of any compensation schemes, the team should be penalized for defective products returned.

Shipping Team's Responsibility and Authority

1. The shipping team responsibility is to ship product as quickly as possible within the limits of shipping rates and authorized overtime.
2. Target is to ship all orders landing on the shipping dock by the end of the day.
3. Inventory for international shipments must not block operations.

Rationale

Packaging and conveyance to the shipping area should be the manufacturing team's responsibility. Shipping team is responsible for special palletizing requirements, arranging shipment, and loading and unloading.

Metric: The weight of unshipped products delivered before 3:00 PM that remains in the shipping area at the close of day.

Plant Engineer's Responsibility and Authority

1. Responsible for providing a safe and efficient work-space
2. Responsible for providing teams with resources to generate product to meet or exceed goals and as safely as possible
3. Must work with plant manager, scheduler and supervisor to continually improve operations
4. Must maintain projected twelve-month capacity between 70 and 80 percent

Rationale

Companies need to invest in equipment to support single-piece flows, to keep manufacturing spaces manageable and load-balance individual tasks. Chaos is reduced by having a single group responsible for all steps in production and eliminating white space.

Metric: Overall plant speed as measured by product produced over a given period.

Plant Manager's Responsibility and Authority

1. Ensures company has enough competent managers and operators for the projected twelve months
2. Ensures all resources are used effective and safely
3. Maintains a strong and ongoing 5Ss program

Metrics: Number of lost time accidents, Grade on 5Ss and safety

CHAPTER 8

Use A3 Thinking

John Shook brings a powerful Japanese practice alive in his book, *Managing to Learn: Using A3 management to solve problems, gain agreement, mentor and lead*.[17] The term A3 refers to a piece of paper roughly 11.7 inches by 16.6 inches. I use 11 inches by 17 inches, which is readily available in the United States. A3 paper is large enough to capture a large project but small enough to force us to think clearly. Why put your thoughts on a single piece of paper? You may improve something that adds little value to the business or jump in with the wrong solution. Consider how most of us usually solve problems versus A3 Thinking.

Figure 12   Human Nature versus A3 Thinking

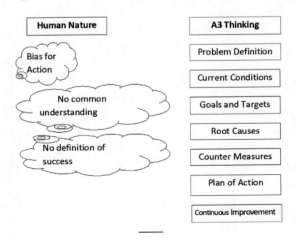

The Way We Think and A3 Thinking

A3 is a problem solving technique that asks us to think through a process. Figure 12 outlines A3 Thinking. While I cannot duplicate A3 paper in this book, here is an example of using A3 thinking:

An Example of A3:
Assess Way Forward to Reduce Lead Times

A3 Title: Reduce median lead-times from eight to four days

As we argued previously, companies gain competitive advantage with quick response to customers. We are losing that advantage as we grow. As a start-up, we routinely provided forty-eight-hour lead times. As we grew, we push capacity into chaos and lead times grew exponentially. Our smaller competitors are starting to beat us. If our lead times have quadrupled since start-up, what will happen if we double the volume again?

Current Condition

Most jobs are completed in less than a half day. Why does it take eight days to ship? It is difficult to quantify business lost because we are losing our competitive advantage.

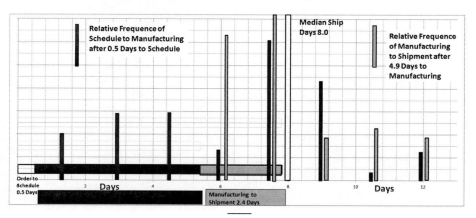

Figure 13 Histogram of Days between Tasks as Tracked over Two Weeks for Multiple Products

Goals/Targets

Reduce lead times from eight to four days. Once product is scheduled, it takes 4.9 days to manufacture. It sits 2.4 days before it ships. Our goal is to produce parts in three days, and ship in one. While it is hard to quantify competitive advantage, we know it has generated millions of dollars in the past. We believe the future holds even greater rewards for being able to respond to customers.

Analysis (Root Causes)

1. Why does it take 4.9 days from schedule to manufacture? Answer: WIP sits while we transfer responsibility or priorities change.
2. Why do we transfer responsibility and change priorities? Answer: No one person or one team is held responsible for completing a job.
3. Why do not we hold one person or team responsible? Answer: We are organized by function.
4. Why are we organized by function? Answer: We started that way.

Solution: Organize by cells.

Other benefits of cellular manufacturing are the following:

1. Reduce space required for large orders by more than half. Allows us to grow without spreading out even further.
2. Employees gain satisfaction from making complete products.
3. One worker can do multiple jobs if we shape the cell in a horseshoe. Generally, cellular manufacture reduces labor requirements.

Countermeasures

1. Form teams to complete jobs. Use packagers on the production line rather than in a shipping department.
2. Move key line to single-piece flow. Spend money on equipment to load level rather than on labor, inventory, or more workspace.
3. Add a second line to ensure short lead times with emergency orders or peak loads. The second line also affords load leveling with single worker handling multiple tasks.

4. Give the scheduler the sole responsibility for on-time delivery; his tools are "how and when" he releases work orders and his authority to authorize over time.
5. Require one team to run production uninterrupted rather than break a current job to run an emergency; have the scheduler move the emergency to the next available team. Build excess equipment and personnel.
6. Measure and compensate employees based on the speed that they deliver finished parts to shipment or finished goods storage.

Plan

Table 5 Steps Required

What?	Who?	When?
Start team meetings to get employees involved with continuous improvement	Scheduler / Supervisors	
Start packaging at the end of production	Scheduler / Supervisors	
Teach team A virtues of single piece flow (SPF)	Master Black Belt	
Define how lines can operate in SPF	Plant Engineer	
Define where new lines are to be located	Plant Engineer	
Layout new SPF lines on the floor and cost needed equipment	Plant Engineer/Supervisors	
Train team in SPF	Supervisors	
Install new equipment	Plant engineer	
Begin measuring speed of production (cycle times)	Supervisors	
Reorganize from functional to cellular; make teams responsible for getting parts ready for shipment	Supervisors	

Follow-up

1. Use control charts to measure impact of change on lead times
2. Meet weekly to keep improvement a daily activity
3. Incorporate metrics into compensation plan

Ask employees for input on continuous improvement

Now imagine this handwritten on a 17-inch by 14-inch piece of paper. Note we clearly define the opportunity. We quantify the current costs and opportunity profit. We define the gap between where we are today in lead times (eight days) to where we need to be (four days). We use *five whys* to find root causes. See chapter 12 for other problem solving techniques. We laid out action, responsibilities, and dates. Most programs omit follow up only to watch the exercise fade and disappear.

CHAPTER 9

5Ss

Five Ss have been widely implemented by large Western firms. Some of my clients called 5S's housekeeping... but it is much more powerful than that. 5S is the first discipline in any improvement. You cannot improve a moving target. Before you can improve, you must standardize what you are doing and clear impediments. 5Ss has been a Japanese staple. The best description of 5Ss was published in Japanese in 1990 as *5s Shidō Manyuaru* and later in English as *5 Pillars of the Visual Workplace: The Sourcebook for 5S Implementation* by Hiroyuki Hirano.[18] Most people use an English *S* as a counter to the original Japanese. I find some of the translations for the sake of using an *S* awkward and rather use the direct translation as presented in *5 Pillars*. While I use the *S* translations, go back to the original translations for meaning.

Table 6 Definitions for 5S

5S	English Translation	Definition	Rationale
Seiri	Organization Sort	Determine what is needed and what to discard	Reduces office or factory footprint
			Eliminates "looking for" time
		If in doubt, through it out	Eliminates obsolescence
			Prevents damages from excessive movement
			Eliminates excessive movement waste
Seiton	Orderliness Set in Order	Organizing so that anyone can find and use things easily	Saves time
			Uses the correct tool
			Easy to see what is missing
Seiso	Cleanliness Sweep	Keep workplace clean and in order	Easily see leaks or if something is missing
			Helps focus deskwork
			Keeps work moving
Seiketsu	Standardize	Standardize clean up	Process to keep first 3S's in place
			Makes 3S's a habit
			Prevents mistakes and damages
			Error proof
Shitsuki	Discipline Sustain	Always follow standardized procedures	Institutionalize 5S Reviews
			Incentivize preventing backsliding

Seri—Sort

One hundred percent of times that I have introduced Sort, I have shop floor employees welcome the opportunity. One hundred percent of the time I have introduced *Seiri* to office workers, I get resistance. Shop workers invariably notice going home in the evening less stressed. They no longer have to interrupt their work rhythms by having to find tools or supplies. We first choose shop floor workers or office workers in each area to red tag items in their work area that are not used daily. Figure 14 is a typical red tag for the factory floor. You can copy the tag on heavy red paper, two to a page. I punch a hole at the top and purchase spools of green garden wire from a garden store to tie the tag.

Figure 14 Red Tag

RED TAG

General Information
Date:_____ Tagged By:_____
Item Name: _____
Quantity:_____ Other ID _____

Category
☐ Equipment   ☐ New Tires
☐ Tools & Jigs   ☐ Tubes
☐ Instruments   ☐ Used Tires
☐ Consumable   ☐ Boxes
☐ Machine Parts   ☐ Other

Reason for Red Tag
☐ Not Required   ☐ Old/Obsolete
☐ Defective   ☐ Other
☐ Scrap

Action
☐ Return to _____
☐ Discard
☐ Move to Red Tag Storage Area
☐ Other

Table 7 Keys for Disposition of Items

Frequency of Use	Disposition
Everyday	Put at arm's length reach
Once a week	Store nearby but away from arm's length
Once a month	On-site but completely out of work area
Once a year	Store off site
Less often than once a year	Get rid of it

While those using their workspace daily should do the tagging, I usually have supervisors oversee actual disposition. We use the rules in Table 7 for disposition of tagged items.

While we remove junk, we do not overlook the need to stock tools and supplies in our work area. We use runners to restock regularly. We eliminate search time.

Seiton—Set in Order

The machine operator must know what normal operation of his equipment sounds like or when leaks are unusual. An office worker needs to know his priorities by what is on his desk. Both shop and office workers need to be able to focus without having to wade through junk.

Orderliness is "a place for everything and everything in its place." I have heard stories about clients outlining where their stapler went. While that may be over the top, we do use visual cues wherever possible. We paint areas where we want to park our idle forklifts. We shadow tools to indicate location. Workers should have everything they use daily within reach in their workspace. If possible, we drop hand tools from overhead beams to be readily available.

In the cloud concept with workers using a common file, there is little excuse for hand carrying paperwork. We can even use electronic decision rules to screen who sees what and to eliminate reviews on less complicated jobs. If a tool is too expensive to have at every workstation, the worker who takes the tool needs to leave her workspace's designation. One company used colored washers on hooks to indicate where missing diagnostic equipment is. We calculate the cost in lost workflow versus buying equipment for every team. We use intracompany e-mail or radios for instant communication. Entry-level runners should replenish supplies and inventory. We use visual cues wherever possible to ensure all equipment is ready to operate. We keep inventory and supplies at a one-day use rate to avoid clutter. The two-bin system works well. We use the left bin to exhaustion, switch, and then replenish the right. If paper work is our inventory, have a runner keep it flowing. Better, get rid of the paper. Do not allow work to stop, but keep excesses out. Keep key workers at their stations and eliminate their clutter.

Seiso—Sweep

Cleanliness means keeping floors and desks spotless. Luxury auto dealers paint their repair shop floors. I have found the best-run truck repair shops have clean, painted floors. It not only shouts to customers that we are the top dealer, mechanics take more pride in their work. *Seiso* also requires inspections. We go through steps to ensure cleanliness:

1. Assign people to targets
    a. Work spaces
    b. Equipment
    c. Traffic areas
2. Clean all areas initially
3. Take pictures and post them as our new standard
4. Keep areas to standard every minute; allocate the last five minutes of the day to audit your work area

Seiketsu—Standardize

We cannot improve a constantly changing process, we cannot quantify waste in a random process, we cannot measure defects and errors with a highly varying process, and teamwork is impossible if everyone uses his own standard. Before attempting to understand or improve any process, standardize.

To standardize is to create a consistent way we do a task. If we have an ISO system, we use it and update it as we improve. Many midsize companies attain ISO standards because it is required for international business. Even though there are ongoing requirements, many companies view maintaining their ISO standards as paper work rather than an opportunity to improve.

Shitsuki—Sustain

I have encountered "here we go again with the flavor of the month." Failure to institutionalize Sustain makes it a "flavor of the month." 3S is not spring-cleaning.

The original translation of *Shitsuki* is discipline. Senior managers teach discipline by setting the example. Companies need to employ regular 5S audits. Schools fix broken windows quickly over the summer to minimize more broken windows. We set expectations. The reward for sustaining 5Ss is not only corporate improvement but employees prefer working in a clean and orderly environment. I have had auto mechanics tell me how much they prefer their new order. They go home less stressed.

Chapter 10

Kaizen Events

Lean Six Sigma covers three formal comprehensive programs Six Sigma, Lean and PDCA. These disciplines borrow heavily from TQM, theory of constraints, Henry Ford, and many others. We find it difficult to convince most small to midsize businesses to support a six-plus month program and use a high percentage of their resources. Six Sigma often requires an outside Black Belt part-time, an inside Black or Green belt full-time, and four to six employees at least two hours a week for six months. To change corporate culture, to improve quality, and to ensure you are working on the right problem with the true root-cause solutions, we would prefer a full Six Sigma project. On the other hand, Six Sigma improves product or service quality as defined by customers, but falls short on improving lead times and reducing costs. Lean is all about shortening the time between the customer order and delivery. We simplify processes and reduce wastes to reduce time; the unvarying effect is to improve quality and reduce costs. Lean uses kaizen events over three to five days, but requires extensive work in pre-event preparation and post-event implementation. Often we implement Lean in two to three months. For perspective, I added a third alternative: Shewhart's and Deming's Plan Do Check (Study) Act or PDCA. PDCA is a iterative process of planning, anticipating results, doing, comparing results to what you expected then adjusting for further improvement. PDCA is the scientific method. We can incorporate PDCA in the other two approaches. While it is easier to justify a Kaizen on a timing and resource basis, Lean can miss the mark. Lean starts by assuming we know what the problem is. It does not involve the enterprise or recommend cultural changes. Lean does not formally query customers upfront. We incorporate Lean and some of the lean deficiencies in the A3 process as described in Table 8.

Table 8 Comparison Among Improvement Programs

Six Sigma	A3 for Kaizen Event	PDCA
Define: Write and get approval of project charter. Validate VOC. Limit scope. Financial benefits	**Title:** Be specific and ensure you are working on the correct problem. **Background:** Why are we doing this? Limit scope.	Plan new project or reset plan on old project. Explain why. Prepare Action Plan
Measure: Value- Stream Map Process Map Gather Data Determine Process Capabilities	**Current Conditions:** What's the problem? What's it costing us? **Goals:** What can we gain? What's the gap between today and future?	Do: Gather Data Analyze Facts Develop Solutions
Analyze: What are critical inputs (the x's in f(x) = y) What are Root Causes? Reduce list of Root Causes to critical few. Estimate impact of the critical few on the output.	**Analysis:** What are the root causes? Choose simplest tool to show cause and effect.	
Improve: Develop solutions. Complete future map. Implement solution. Confirm goal attainment.	**Propose Countermeasures:** Your proposal. How do you think countermeasures will impact the root cause to achieve the goal? **Plan:** List activities, dates and responsibilities required for implementation. What are indicators of progress?	Check: Test solutions Ensure Goals are satisfied Implement Solutions
Control: Mistake proof process Develop SOP's Continue to improve with control charts and other metrics Turn process over to operators	**Follow-up:** Continue measuring Discuss in weekly meetings Relate how reaching goal helps the company reach its ultimate financial goal	Act: Monitor Solutions Continuous Improvement

We should complete a 5S program on the process that we choose before planning a kaizen event. See chapter 9. Pay particular attention to standardization. We must have the process in control before studying it. Put another way, we cannot change a moving target. Identify the person, team or equipment that generates the highest quality product or service in the shortest time. Benchmark and apply the best methods at every workstation.

At least one week ahead of the kaizen event we conduct a training session. I would recommend supplying team members with this book and discuss value stream mapping (VSM). The goal of a VSM is to visualize on paper a complex process and identify areas for improvement. Create templates to record times for each task. There are dozens of VSM templates on the internet. Naming the problem is not trivial. The name should reflect the project scope. Be specific in what you want achieved. That is, "provide room service from guest call to food delivery in less than thirty minutes". Note I defined the measurement. On the other hand, keep scope limited. Scope creep is one of the major causes for project failure. Follow the A3 template. Consider the A3 example in chapter 8. Gather historical data to define the current state.

The purpose of a kaizen event is to eliminate waste. You should choose a process that has a reasonable combination as having the highest potential for waste reduction yet can be improved in three to six months without a major investment. It is critical that the board or owners are supportive. The team should consist of the following:

- Kaizen leader, often a Black Belt
- Process owner, often a supervisor
- Four to six employees that work on the process daily

Ideally, you should block off five working days, where team employees are considered on vacation. In practice with small to midsize companies, I can often find it possible only to get six to eight people for three days at a time. We work with the resources we have.

What do we do in pre-event? Find a team meeting room close to the *gemba* or shop floor that we will study. We need lots of wall space to trace every process step and a large table. Preplanning is key to success. Have a plan and agenda. Set up a direct line with owners or a senior project champion in case we hit a snag or need resources. Have a communication plan between the team, the project champion, and workers who are not on the team. In the plan, state expectations and post ground rules.

The first day, we review the pre-training and 5Ss. Each team member needs:

1. pencils and paper,
2. a stopwatch,
3. comfortable shoes, and
4. a video camera.

Everyone must tour the *gemba* to grasp the entire process. Map backward from the customer's perspective. Working backward can stimulate right-brain thinking and "seeing" the whole process. We use a video camera to delve deeper into a particular task if required.

Follow two streams: the material flow and information flow. Record cycle times and the number of people and amount of material involved at each step. Identify steps that "value add." That is, value add tasks answer answers positively to all four questions:

15   Data Box

Data Box	
Product	
Process:	
Cycle Time	
No. Operators	
No. Shifts	
Batch Size	
Scrap rate	
Avg Queue in minutes	% VA
	% NVA
	% BNVA
Top 3 Causes for Delays	
Top 3 Defects	

Value Add (VA)

1. Does this task change the form or feature to the product or service?
2. Would the customer pay extra for the change?
3. Is it done right the first time?
4. Does the task enable a competitive advantage?

Activities that are not VA are either nonvalue add (NVA) or business nonvalue add (BNA). We should severely reduce or eliminate NVA. BNA are those activities that are required by regulations and cannot be eliminated. We record information about each process in a data box. Please consider buying *Lean Six Sigma Pocket Toolbook* for a more detailed explanation of VSM.[19]

We design the data box according to the process. There are many examples of VSMs and data boxes available on the internet. Figure 15 shows one example that I have used.

After designing the current state, we identify areas for improvement. Then as a team, we design an improved future state. We never use computers for the VSM; it is a waste of resources. We do not expect a perfect current state before designing a future state. If you have a long continuous process, you can include Takt time. Takt time is simply the rhythm of production or the time required to produce one widget or one claim form. For example, we must make one widget every fifteen seconds to meet customer expectations. To calculate Takt time, we divide available work time by customer's demand (number of widgets). From the rhythm, we can load-balance a line. That is, find a combination of steps that a single person or machine can handle to maintain the required rhythm. Takt times define the number of steps. With short-run operations, we cannot use Takt time, but we can find an optimal pace of production that minimizes personnel. We determine the process constraint and feed the constraint continuously. In theory, WIP only builds ahead of the single constraint. In practice, operators relieve stress by having a small reserve in case they need a break. We want to avoid what Lucy and Ethyl encountered at the chocolate factory. If you have no clue what I am talking about, ask someone in his or her fifties about *I Love Lucy*. We add capacity at the constraint if possible. For steps with short cycle times, we combine steps for a single operator as shown in figure 6. That gets back to cross-training personnel. I found one company that had been running a single press to complete two operations. The press was the line's constraint. WIP piled up in front of and between operations. We capped parts on one end, stocked all WIP and recapped the other end reusing a single press. The company had unlimited warehouse spaced and never considered the waste and total process inefficiencies. Capping was the constraint. Duplicating presses in sequence to eliminate the constraint seemed odd. Why?

We review each day's work at the end of the day and revise the following day's agenda. We keep the project champion or owner abreast of daily activity.

Before leaving, we complete as much of the A3 template as possible. Pay particular attention to root causes for key problems. We define what, who, and when to complete the project. We insist on adding sustaining practices to avoid "flavor of the month". Before we close, we celebrate.

CHAPTER 11

Behavioral Change

Push Through the Valley of Despair

Change fails much more often than it exceeds. Think about your New Year's resolutions. Everyone, who tries to change, hits the valley of despair. Winners push through the valley. Why do we resist change?

> People would rather live with a problem they cannot solve than accept a solution they cannot understand. (Robert Woolsey)

Change Individual Behavior by Addressing Why We Resist Change

Changing old habits is much more difficult than adding new ones. I find that everyone needs to dig deep to articulate both what they expect to gain and what is causing them to resist. On a white board, write what you want to change. Draw a line down the middle of the board. On the left side we put all the reasons we need to change. On the right side, we put why we will resist. The resist side requires brutal honesty. You will find multiple descriptions of this process under the heading Force Field Analysis on the internet. See figure 16. Most consultants miss the importance of listing the reasons why we must

Figure 16 Force Field Analysis

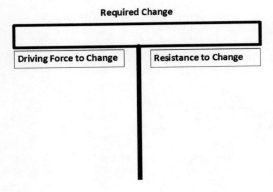

change. Some have called such a listing the Blood Wall. That is, we must change all of those things that have caused us pain. I prefer Opportunity Wall. See table 9. List the realistic opportunities change will offer. You must have driving force to overcome the pain of despair. Leave the opportunity wall up for the duration. Examples of driving forces are the following:

1. Success ensures my retirement.
2. Company will share gains.
3. Increase order in my workspace reduces stress.
4. This specific change will result in . . .

Forces of Resistance often cited, include the following:

1. I feel inadequate to do the new tasks.
2. I fear personal loss.
3. I am not prepared.
4. I fear the unknown.
5. I had no input.

Address each resistance with an action plan to overcome the fear or problem. Including more people in this exercise is better than too few. Pilot change, if possible. Communicate your vision and benefits repeatedly. Keep the opportunity wall up for the duration of the project. Be receptive to bad news without shooting the messenger. Track and communicate improvements.

Most people do not recognize how difficult it is to change an organization. Change fails because our fears and stresses are never surfaced and addressed. You must get people to dig deep to address their real concerns.

Table 9 Opportunity Wall

Improvement	Details	Benefit
Simplify Estimation Process	Benefit: Save 12.5 hrs per wk per estimator	$1,130,000
	Estimate on the spot to preempt the bid process	
	Benefit: Apply save time to sales development	
Simplify Purchasing Process	Benefit: Reduce duplication of effort	$500,000
	Benefit: Reduce errors	
	Benefit: Save 10 hrs per wk	
Improve Sales Closure Rate	Benefit: (25% improvement)	$540,000
Using a plan to ensure success	5-Yr Plan to increase value	$1,000,000
	Forces new thinking; What do have to do to meet goals?	
Improve Productivity	More than 10 percent improvement	
	Focus on eliminating WIP	
	Focus on getting project out door in 24 hrs	
	Work emergency orders into schedule; do not interrupt on-going work	
	40% more productive	
	75% less floor space	
	75% fewer errors	
	75% fewer damages	
Total Potential Savings		**$3,170,000**

Be a Player, Not a Victim

Start by getting everyone in the company to understand that each individual shares responsibility for change. I asked an employee who constantly talked about his daughter's softball prowess:

> "If you were driving your daughter to an important softball tournament but ran into a traffic accident and your daughter was late. As a result, her substitute pitched. Whose fault was it?"

When I ask this question, about half the time, people say, "It was no one's fault." I disagree. If you were there, you were part of the problem. Why did not you leave early to anticipate a traffic problem? Ask every employee to be a player, not a victim. Without employee commitment, change usually fails.

Increase Time Spent on Change

Figure 17   Reducing Fires

	Not Urgent	Very Urgent
Critical	Managing the business Fire prevention Train,	Fire Fighting No time to improve situation Force time
Not Important	Stop doing these things	Delegate phone calls Get out of this Box entirely

Tasks Importance (vertical axis) — **Task Urgency** (horizontal axis)

Callout: It's often better to take a short-term loss in productivity in order to install long term gains

Most managers in small to midsize businesses don many hats. They are generally engrossed in daily operations and have little time to focus on change. The operations manager for multiple auto parts stores personally went to each store to assess inventory for their once-a-year opportunity to return inventory. The manager deemed this highest priority because of cost savings. Every time he would delegate this task, he found the stock puller would miss inventory. Rather than further training, the manager just said, "I'll do it myself." Actually, this is common in midsize businesses. What the manager missed is that by spending a significant time fighting fires rather than training others or pushing down responsibility, the company was incapable of readying itself to grow to the next level.

1. **Urgent and Important (fire fighting).** These are the everyday priorities, things that have either come up urgently, or important things that you did not give attention until they became urgent.
2. **Urgent and Not Important (distraction).** These are the easiest things to move to, but hardly the most productive. Everyone has tasks that fall into this category.
3. **Not Urgent But Important (quality time—fire prevention).** It is creating your strategic vision or planning kaizen events. Use this time to plan and execute. Use this time to prevent fires.
4. **Not Urgent, Not Important (time wasting).** Only do these to reduce stress, then keep it limited.

Settle for the Doable Rather than the Most Logical

George Eckes in his book, *Six Sigma Revolution*, discusses how the *success of a change* is directly related to the product of the *quality of the solutions* and the *acceptance of the solution*.[20] That is, it is sometimes better to modify an improvement program if it means that you can get key stakeholders on board rather than to go with the technically superior plan. Eckes further suggests identifying key stakeholders and targeting their concerns. Even if you have full support from the board or owners, the employees that implement change must be on board. Peripheral stakeholders must at least not undercut your improvement. Direct users must be fully on board, or you will fail. Target key stakeholders and educate or cajole them to a level that supports the improvement.

Conscientiously Incorporate a Mechanism for Continuous Improvement

Modern improvement technologies, such as Lean Six Sigma and Demings's Plan Do Study Act, have a strong basis in classical scientific method. Six Sigma requires enterprise commitment up to the board level and insists on incorporating a mechanism for continuous improvement.

I often hear, when I am introduced to employees, "here comes another flavor of the month." Most companies have gone through multiple self-help programs. Often, people see the value but never fully own it. Change takes time and repetition. In studies of mice, it took twenty-one repetitions to incorporate a new habit. It seems to be a good rule for humans as well. Therefore, most change programs require a strong catalyst for at least six months to create lasting change.

For long-term change, we need to incorporate continuous improvement. I find that incorporating control charts and continuous tracking a strong catalyst to instill change. Control charts have built in mechanisms to detect significant change, both positive and negative. By concurrently tracking all activity associated with the metric, we can associate cause and effect. Repeat the good activity; eliminate or modify the bad. There are other ways to continuously improve. Using variance analysis on drilled down accounts, job costing, etc., are easy accounting measures. Everything should be compared to stretch goals. We often develop a rating scale for employing the 5Ss in the front office and shop floor. Developing contingency plans in advance and monitoring trigger points is another good technique. We insist on formal weekly reviews focused on data to keep programs alive.

Chapter 12

Problem Solving

Recently, a small company asked me to develop the position of general manager and help recruit someone. On our first meeting with the two owners and an owner's wife, you could feel the tension. The founder of the company and his wife, owner A, were more interested in philanthropic issues and their lack of total immersion in the company left employees uncertain about their responsibilities. Owner A and his wife were concerned about retaining control and they were the ones pushing for a general manager. Clearly, high-level duties were left unattended and a new general manager could take up these duties. The other owner, Owner B, was working ten hours a day and felt he was responsible for the company's recent good growth. He felt bringing on board someone who was not intimately familiar with his business would be disruptive. Further, he did all the work, and owner A took the same draws and salary. Everyone would lose if the issue were not resolved. Owner B threatened to quit. The problem illustrates what most of us face on a daily basis, a dilemma. Rather than addressing the underlying root causes, we argue over the symptoms.

After a long discussion, I noted how all scheduling and contact to customers went through owner B. Rather than groom an outside general manager, I worked to improve the companies operation by pushing scheduling down to newly organized teams. As a result, owner B could attend to high-level duties. We restructure the ownership to allow owner A to retain voting rights, but owner B had all authority for day-to-day operations. We separated definitions, duties and pay for employee-owner and owner only. We paid the owner-employee as an employee, yet the owners split dividends according to ownership. By making their operation cellular and giving more responsibility to teams, the business could break its "organization" ceiling and grow.

There several techniques to look through points of contention to underlying causes. Dr. Eliyahu M. Goldratt calls his process, evaporating clouds. It is one of the six thinking processes in the theory of constraints.[16] Evaporating clouds take emotion out of your conflict and focuses on underlying needs rather than the points of contention. Let us take another look at the emotional issue concerning whether or not to hire a general manager.

The Evaporating Cloud creates new solutions. Thus, it has an infinite number of possible outcomes. Goldratt's Evaporating Cloud model assumes that both parties in a conflict must share a common goal. If they do not share a goal, there is no need for the conflict, so both sides could walk away from it. The heart of the Evaporating Cloud process is to convert the situation from "me versus you" to "you and me against the problem."

The process starts with blocks "Hire a GM" and "Do not hire a GM"—the two opposing positions that define the conflict. These can be in the form of X versus Not X, or in the form of X versus Y. Next, you work to identify the common goal that both sides of the conflict share. This common goal is block "Improve control of company."

The second step involves having each opposing sides to define *why* for their position. That is, the need that they are trying to satisfy with their position. Consider the following statements:

> "In order to have more control, we must have must hire a GM."
> "In order to not disrupt the company, we cannot hire a GM."

Figure 18 Evaporating Cloud

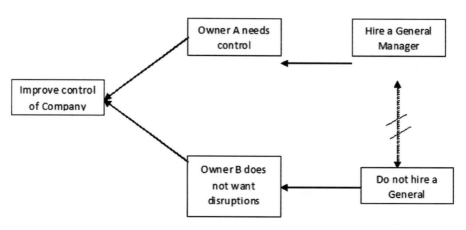

The solution was not about hiring a GM. It was the about control. The solution to bridge the underlying motivation was to improve the manufacturing operation so that owner B has more time to attend higher-level company operations and to change the structure of ownership to satisfy owner A.

Figure 19 Resolved Evaporating Cloud

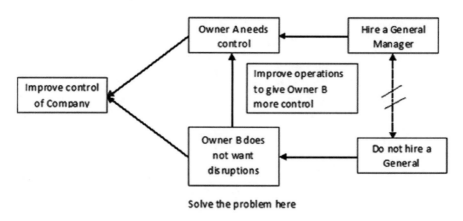

Five *Whys*

The Japanese use the five *why*s. We use five *why*s when our group faces a seemingly intractable problem. It is what we did as kids: keep asking why.
Why do we need five *why*s?

1. The immediate problem may be too broad or amorphous to propose a solution or
2. The immediate obvious solution may be an effect and not a root cause or
3. The immediate solution is too difficult to quantify.

When do we stop asking why? (It may not take five questions).

1. When we reached a solution that positively satisfies the deficiencies listed above or
2. When we reach a solution that is beyond the teams skill set or resources to resolve or
3. When the questions start broadening rather than narrowing the solutions.

Examples of Five *Whys*

Example 1

Problem: We were put on credit alert.

1. Why were we put on credit hold from our supplier? Because we did not pay our bills.
2. Why didn't we pay our bills? The invoice was not processed.
3. Why wasn't the invoice processed? The invoice did not show up in the system.
4. Why didn't the invoice show up in the system? Because our system requires us to create a demand before we create an order.
5. Why did we not create a demand before we create an order? Because a branch store did not follow the protocol.

Solution: Set up a ***written protocol*** that the store sales must follow when entering an order.

Example 2

Problem: Customers wait too long for the operator to answer and choose other providers.

1. Why do customers wait too long? There are times when we have too many calls to handle effectively.
2. Why can't we handle calls at peak times? We do not have enough operators.
3. Why do we not have enough operators? We set the number of operators by the average number of calls . . .
4. Why do we set the number of operators by the average? That is the way we have always done it.

Solution: Staff for peak and nonpeak hours. Stagger our phone operator's hours.

Example 3

Problem: We are regularly ordering from the highest cost supplier.

1. Why are regularly ordering from the highest cost supplier? The wrong supplier was selected.
2. Why was the wrong supplier selected? Not all suppliers show on my computer screen.
3. Why was not the correct supplier on your screen? Because I had to scroll down to see them.
4. Why did you have to scroll down to see them? It was programmed that way.

Solution: Reprogram the screen to include all critical suppliers.

Tools to Solve Complex Problems: Speak with Data

If the problem is complex, use A3 thinking. There are several tools that all managers should be familiar to analyze data and find relations between variables:

Traditional Western Tools

1. Histograms
2. Flow charts
3. Control charts
4. Regressive analysis
5. Hypothesis testing
1. Design of experiments[21]

Management tools developed by Nayatani in Japan in 1982

1. Tree diagrams
2. Matrix diagrams
3. Activity network diagrams
4. PDPC charts
5. Affinity diagrams
6. Interrelation matrixes
7. Prioritization matrixes

Tools help visualize relations and test for significance. Every company should have someone familiar with these tools. Again, I would suggest buying Michael George et al *Lean Six Sigma Pocket Toolbook* as a start.[20] The best way to attain the tools is to encourage leaders to become Green Belts in Lean Six Sigma. I use these tools at nearly every business whether manufacturing or service. Your company could be in jeopardy if you lack basic tools that allow you to see critical relations.

The concept of probing for root causes is similar to how top companies use SPIN Selling techniques. SPIN is an acronym coined by Neil Rackham in 1988.[22] I draw the comparison because both SPIN Selling and the problem solving techniques discussed above require asking extensive questions to find the underlying issues. Selling by quoting features and benefits is about as ineffective as immediately solving a problem by looking at symptoms rather than root causes. In both cases, we need to first ask questions and avoid offering solutions. One client told his consultant, "Make my life easier and the money will follow." The consultant persisted with her sales pitch about how much money she would make for my client and lost the consulting engagement. It's not about you. Listen first. I love the irony that competent problem solvers fail to heed their own advice.

When we identify the root cause, we should literally and figuratively step around the table and work on solving the problem together. In my sales seminars I tell my students *not* to revert to "my company can . . . ," but rather stick with "if we do this, we can . . ." Keep the customer in the solution. When resolving a conflict, stay with "we can . . ." Similarly, two antagonists that use evaporating clouds to resolve a dilemma should stay on the same side of the table to work the solution. As an aside, do you notice I use *we*? I do so to keep my reader involved. Further, using first-person pronouns keeps me in active voice and makes reading this book easier.

Get an Assist from the Right Brain

I have referred to right-brain thinking. The right brain hides from most of us, particularly engineers and accountants. We think in words, using logic, and in sequence to solve problems. Often we miss the obvious or the radical. That is where we should seek a right-brain assist. Betty Edwards in her book *The New Drawing on the Right Side of the Brain* compares the two sides of the brain.[23] Some of her findings are summarized in Table 10. Seeing what should be retards our ability to see what is. She has her students reproduce drawings upside-down. In an upside-down view, it is more difficult for our left brain to tell us what should be. Two dimensions flatten what we expect. Our left brain does not see long staircases getting smaller as we look up. She also uses a viewfinder help us to see in perspective. Her students use a sheet of glass with one vertical and one horizontal line crossing in the middle. By relating the distance in our glass viewfinder from the centerlines, we can recreate realistic representation of our hands with fingers curled toward the viewfinder. Before using these techniques to see relations, we substitute logic for reality. Fingers do not get fatter as they point to your eyes as logic tells us. In analyzing data, I consider statistics as the viewfinder telling us what is real.

Table 10 Left Brain versus Right Brain

Left Brain	Right Brain
Thinks in words	Perceives emotions, facial expressions, body language, tone of voice
Processes logically	Processes the whole or sees underlying relations
Thinks sequentially	Thinks out of sequence or in aggregate
Uses symbols or substitutes for what we expect rather than what is	See things as they are
Building blocks form a house	Recognizes the house immediately

Ms. Edwards specifically warns us not to say, "This is a nose or this is an ear." She wants us to suppress the left brain that thinks in words and symbols. I suspect my readers are skeptical at this point. Either take my word for how not naming a nose allows you the actually draw what you see or buy Betty Edwards's book and see for yourself. People whose right and left brains have been split were shown one object to their right eye (left brain) and another to their left eye (right brain). Left brain would shout out its object's name, while concurrently, the right brain would shake his head emphatically no.[24] Fortunately, most of us can coax the right and left brain to work together. Working backward in value stream mapping helps to visualize what is, rather than what should be. *Eureka*s come in dreams or times we turn our logical mind off.

While most of us do not aspire to be a famous artist, we do aspire to have more eureka moments. It is at the point of elation when we say "I get it" or "It all comes together." Those are clear indication that we broke through the trees to see the forest. Those are right-brain moments. I take key problems to bed to induce eureka moments. I try to view the future in pictures and suppress words and order. As a consultant, I find myself looking down every avenue for answers. I purposefully avoid drawing conclusions until the last moment. Often, adrenalin brings it home. From leaving my desk to the whiteboard in front of clients, I put it together. I have been thinking of this book for years. Before starting, I was all over the place. When I sat down to write the book, it flowed continuously. I did, however, use my left brain over weeks to make my words make sense.

One way to draw eureka moments is to brainstorm. Define a problem and have people close to the problem shout-out ideas. Do not allow anyone to defend his or her positions. Keep it crisp. Do not critique. Encourage rapid-fire solutions. Suspend logic. After the well runs dry, group solutions by similarity. Only allow people to clarify their ideas, but again, not to defend. Have people vote on the best solutions. As rule of thumb, divide the total number of people by three and allow everyone to use the division answer rounded up number of votes. That is, if there are seventeen people in the brainstorming section, allow everyone to cast six votes. Use Pareto's eighty-twenty rule to select options to pursue.

As a scientist, I find it hard not to defend my position at the brainstorming stage. Even voting on solutions without talking through each one seems strange. Brainstorming works by separating the best solutions. By having multiple votes, people work through solutions without groupthink. Once the top solutions are selected, we do defend, analyze and prioritize. Brainstorming invites the radical without stopping at the first logical solution. One cleaver and articulate person does not cut short ideas. Nor does group enthusiasm dissuade further thought.

Sometimes Simple is a Magical Cure

The simplest solution to avoid mistakes is to use a checklist. Checklists are so simple that most of us never think about using them. Pilots walk around their planes with a checklist. Race drives walk their cars before a race. They repeat the walk-around thousands of times even though they know the drill by heart. Why use a checklist? I had taken several thousand trips forgetting something critical about 10 percent of the time. That would give me a C minus on the six sigma scale and worse on my wife's stupidity scale. See table 11. After twenty years of living with travel panic, I put a checklist in my wallet. I now pull out the yellowing list in figure 20 and stand by car, checking off each item. In ten years with this card, I have never left any critical item. When I show this list to my clients, they question my senility. When counter clerks use their admittedly mindless lists, they are shocked at how their checklist eliminates forgetting to include freight on invoices or open a demand before a purchase order (as when a clerk in a distribution company forgets to enter a customer's order before ordering it from a primary vendor). Computers have internal lists that do not allow us to forget important items. Lists are simple but often the only practical solutions.

Figure 20 Travel Check List.

```
Travel Check List Critical and Previous Left Items
Brief Case:
        Computer
        Computer power supply
        Printer cable
        Printer
        Printer power supply
Suit Case
        Belt
        Suit pants
Medicine Bag
        Black diabetes kit
Cell phone
GPS
Wallet
        American Express card
        Driver's license
Ticket
```

Checklists are also powerful tools in collecting data for statistical analysis. Statisticians prefer continuous data such as grams, inches, etc. Think of continuous data as being divisible. Dividing five grams by two leaves a legitimate amount—two and a half grams. I find discrete data such as reason lists useful as well. We cannot divide discrete data such as yes or no or five people by two. No, we do not count a child as a half person. Grocery stores check off a list of reasons every time it takes more than four minutes to check out. My machine shop lists reasons for delays. My limousine client checked off reason lists for complaints. Reason lists, though simple, can be powerful analytical tools.

I emphasize checklists because they are so simple, and most people go years without thinking of them.

Solve Problems and Quality from the Front End

Figure 21 Time to Resolve Defects Grows Exponentially the Further Downstream

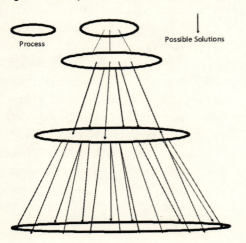

In total quality management, we learned to push quality as far back in the manufacturing process as possible. If we can error proof every step, final inspection is a waste of time. Solving problems fits the same model.

In many respects, pushing resolution upstream is a subset of asking the five *why*s. I have had repair shops spend hours a day per person trying to figure out who ordered a part. In figure 21, that would be analogous to trying to solve a problem at the third level. We had to retrace all movement. The second level was the distributor. We ultimate resolved the problem by incorporating our work-order number through the distributor to the primary vendor. The problem was resolved at our vendor's vendor's level. We pushed the solution as far upstream as possible.

Change Our Culture from Accepting Problems to Solving Problems as They Arise

In many companies, managers have worked in their area for many years. They know everything. Often I see employees making the same mistakes repeatedly. The managers, after a few harsh words to their employees, do it themselves. It is shocking how many companies accept repeating the same mistakes. The mere act of looking at processes triggers a cultural change. At an auto parts store, I overheard employees discussing how they could reduce inventory offs. These employees had been pulling inventory for thirty years. Previously, when managers discovered inventory that was misplaced, they blamed the stockers or pullers. The company relied on people to read product codes. I looked at rows of yellow boxes of the same size. They had six digit codes, differing in some cases by a middle digit. For example, two parts would have codes 8AM554 and 8AM654 respectively. One was put on one shelf, the other on a shelf in the next column of shelves. The best stocker will make tens of mistakes per thousand. Rather than trying to train stockers to be more accurate, one stocker suggested they use their barcode guns to pull and restock. Inventory offs dropped. Once the company understood they could not train to an acceptable level, they consider improving their methods. The most productive ideas began to erupt from stockers. Managers had wasted their worker available brainpower for thirty years.

Table 11 Rating Company Performance by Mistakes or Defects per Opportunity

Performance Grade	Sigma Level	Mistakes per million opportunities	Mistakes per 1000 opportunities	Mistakes per 100 opportunities
A plus	6	3.4	0.003	0.0003
A	5	233	0.23	0.02
B	4	6,219	6.2	0.6
C	3	66,811	67	6.7
D	2	308,770	309	31

World class operations only have 3.4 defects per million opportunities. Most people think that is a ridiculously high standard. Is it? Put it in real life. If the fifty million take offs and landings in the United States in 2011 crashed 3.4

times per million, we would have 172 crashes. Is 3.4 per one million really too high? Further, we multiply probabilities for mistakes or defects. Think of the thousands of components on chips in modern electronics. If manufacturers accepted one defect per hundred components, we would still be in the vacuum tube era where ENIAC calculated pi to 2,037 digits. Modern computers calculate pi to fifty-one billion decimal places. It is a more complex world.

The point is that most US companies operate between a two and three Sigma level. That is, they accept between six and thirty-one mistakes per hundred opportunities. I had parts people that had no confidence in their parts database. They would leave their phone and counter to verify their inventory before committing to an order over the phone. The company was in a competitive market and every time a phone went unanswered, the customer would call a competitor. We tracked inventory offs and found about five offs for every one hundred inquiries. Every time a counter person mistakenly commits to a customer, either we lose a customer, or we pay for airfreight. Each mistake gets a manager and a salesperson involved. I asked, "How many times a week are we having mistakes currently?" The answer came back, two to three times a day. We confirmed that by statistics. I asked, "What could we live with?" They felt that once every two weeks would keep the turmoil in check. We set our goal to one mistake every two thousand inquiries. That would make us nearly a B company. We could not justify the effort to go beyond four Sigma. We went from inventory offs per hundred to inventory offs per two thousand. These statistics take into account that our process ebbs and flows with the level of activity, introducing new people, etc. The fluctuations are called sigma shifts.

Also in our business culture, managers must push back on employees or vendors that say no to a request. I always insist that employees tell me alternatives or substantiate "no." I once asked one of the largest cable operators in the United States why they keep coming back to my client to install cable. My client was a start-up on a shoestring. His company was quadrupling in size every year in a slow market. The engineer for the national cable company told me that my client never says no. If what the cable company request was unworkable, my client found alternatives. I am shocked at how often managers accept no.

My conclusion is that most companies accept no and mistakes without follow up or question. This attitude is endemic in small to mid-sized companies. They cannot become world class until every employee asks, "how can we improve or avoid this mistake?" or "are there alternatives?" Management has to encourage this attitude. By institutionalizing questioning mistakes or looking for alternatives, we can improve many processes immediately. Others may require a formal A3 inquiry or a full Six Sigma program.

CHAPTER 13

Guide to Prosperity

We started by asking "Is it a scary world". The world lived through difficult times from 2008 through 2010 in what some called the great recession. The world has reordered quickly from the late 1980s where books were published about the coming Japanese century. Then Japan's property value bust hit and the underpinnings of their economy disappeared. China's near vertical growth has flattened. India appears to be reintroducing bureaucracy. Outside of Africa and South America, populations are aging rapidly. The Western world has a short window to accommodate change. We cannot walk away from manufacturing and providing many services. We must find ways to compete. As I have suggested, we will compete by providing better design and being responsive and nibble. Focus on speed of production by optimizing processes.

I give you a little theory and a lot of "how to." The one thought that ties prosperity together is this:

> Get a designed product or service out the door as fast as possible and with as little footprint as possible.

Finally, I talked about expending great effort upfront. Find purpose. Plan. Spend time getting all employees involved in the plan. Communicate. In her new book, *All in: The Education of General David Petraus,* Paula Broadwell relates General Petraeus's four task for strategic thinking as the following:[25]

1. Get the big ideas right.
2. Communicate those big ideas.
3. Implement those big ideas.
4. Capture best practices and lessons and cycle them back through the system to help refine the big ideas.

General Petraeus, perhaps the most effective leader since WWII, encouraged low-level officers to e-mail him with their concerns. He sought input from all levels within his combined forces. Corporations must effectively utilize all of its brain power and involve all levels.

New jobs require workers to participate in improvement programs and teams to work autonomously. American politics is incapable of improving education. Small to midsized companies may have to recruit high-skilled labor from Europe and elsewhere to fill the skills gap in the United States. The average high-skilled industrial worker in the United States is in their mid-fifties. We must find room for apprentices to replace aging workers. Future CEOs will increasingly see themselves as working for their employees.

INDEX

A

A3. *See* A3 thinking
A3 thinking, 58–59, 84
Activity Based Accounting, 43

B

brainstorm, 87
buffers, 49
business, project-oriented, 50

C

capacity utilization, reduction without capital, 45
cellular offices, 40
cellular operations, 25, 39
cellular organizations, 24
change, behavioral, 73
change over, 24, 36–37, 53
chaos, 22, 38, 40–43, 45, 59
Collins, Jim, 19
compassion, misplacing of, 42
Conceptual Age, 12, 19–20

control charts, 27–28, 62, 78
Critical Chain Project Management, 49–50
cross-training, 32, 72

D

data box, 71
deliveries, on-time, 40
doable, settle for the, 77
dream think, 52

E

efficiency, focusing on, 43
80 percent capacity, 42
envelopes, stuffing of, 31
error proof, 32, 88
eureka moments, 86
Evaporating Clouds, 80, 85

F

fire fighting, 77
fire prevention, 77

5 S. *See* 5*S*s
5, 63
Five *S*s. *See* 5*S*s
Five *Why*s, 82, 88
five-Year Plan, 19
Force Field Analysis, 73–74

G

gemba, 70–71
goals, 24

H

human talent, waste of unused, 25

I

improvement, continuous, 40, 62, 77–78
insight, loss of, 50, 52
inventory offs, 89
ISO standards, 67

J

Joe (the plumber), 46, 48

K

kaizen events, 68–70

L

lead times, reducing, 40, 99
Lean Six Sigma, 13, 29
Little's Law, 35
load-balance, 56, 72

M

metrics, 25, 27–28, 57
multiply supervision, 25
multitasking, 50–53

O

opportunity, loss of, 50, 52
opportunity crossing preparations, 16
Opportunity Wall, 74–75

P

PDCA (plan do check act), 68
people and equipment, keeping busy, 41
Petraus, General David, 92
problem solving, 79
purpose, 15–16, 21

R

remobilization, 51
reset operations, 54
reverse engineer, 21
right brain, 71, 85–86
root causes, 43, 72, 79, 84–85

S

score card, balanced, 22
Seiketsu (Standardized), 67
Seiso (Sweep), 66
Seiton (Set in Order), 65
Seri (Sort), 64
Shitsuki (Sustain), 67
short runs, 20, 29
single-piece flow, 18, 31–32, 34–35, 39,

49, 56, 60
Six Sigma, 13, 28–29, 68, 71, 77, 84, 91, 100
SMED (Single-Minute Exchange of Die), 12, 36
standard accounting, 43
Suri, Rajan, 13

T

Takt time, 44, 71–72
throughput accounting, 32
traditional accounting, 32

V

VA (value add), 37, 71
variation, 33–34, 50
vision, 17, 22–23, 74, 77
VSM (value stream mapping), 70–71, 86

W

white space, 37, 99
Woolsey, Robert, 73
work flow pipe, 46–47

Y

year one, drill down to, 24

ENDNOTES

1. Thomas Friedman, *The Word Is Flat: A Brief History of the Twenty-First Century* (New York: Piccador 2007).
2. Article #21916 in mfrtech.com, "Bringing It Back Home: The Resurgence of U.S. Manufacturing."
3. Richard Deitz and James Orr, "A Leaner, More Skilled U.S. Manufacturing Workforce", *Current Issues in Economics and Finance* 12, no. 2 (2006).
4. Daniel Pink, *A Whole New Mind: Why Right-Brainers Will Rule the Future* (New York: Penguin Group, 2006).
5. Rajan Suri, *Quick Response Manufacturing: A Companywide Approach to Reducing Lead Times*, 1st ed (New York: Productivity Press, 1998).
   Simon Sinek, *Start with Why: How Great Leaders Inspire Everyone to Take Action* (New York: Portfolio, 2009).
6. Malcolm Gladwell, *Outliers: The Story of Success* (New York: Back Bay Books, 2008).
7. Walter Isaacson, Steve Jobs, Simon & Schuster, New York, 2011.
8. Jim Collins, *Good to Great* (New York: Harper Business, 2001).
9. Rajan Suri, *It's About Time: The Competitive Advantage of Quick Response Manufacturing* (New York: CRC Press, 2010).
10. James Collins and J Porras, *Built to Last* (New York: Harper Business, 2004).
11. James Womack, *Lean Thinking* (Pennsylvania: Pennsylvania State University Free Press, 2003).
12. Raymond Carey and Larry Stake, *Improving Healthcare with Control Charts: Basic and Advanced SPC Methods and Case Studies* (Wisconsin: Quality Press, 2003).
13. White Space and similar diagrams were introduced by Rajan Suri in the aforecited *"It's About time: The Competitive Advantage of Quick Manufacturing"*

14. MCT stands for Manufacturing Critical-Path Time, which is roughly the same thing as lead time that we have described. Lower MCT is lower lead-time.
15. Eliyahu Goldratt, *The Goal*, 3rd ed. (Massachusetts: The North River Press, 2004).
16. Eliyahu M. Goldratt, *Critcal Chain Management*,
17. John Shook, *Managing to Learn* (Massachusetts: The Lean Enterprise, 2008).
18. Hiroyuki Hirano, *5 Pillars of the Visual Workplace: The Sourcebook for 5S Implementation* (New York: The Productivity Press, 1995).
19. Michael George et al, *Lean Six Sigma Pocket Toolbook* (New York: McGraw-Hill, 2005).
20. George Eckes, *Six Sigma Revolution* (New York: John Wiley & Sons, 2001).
21. Design of Experiments (DOE) was developed by Ronald Fisher in 1935; modern DOE is closely associated with Genichi Taguchi.
22. Neil Rackham, *SPIN Selling*, 1st ed. (New York: McGraw-Hill, 1988).
23. Betty Edwards, *The New Drawing on the Right Side of the Brain*, 4th add. (New York: Penguin Putnam Inc., 1999cx).
24. J. Levy, G. Trevarthen and R. Sperry, "Perception of Bilateral Chimeric Figures Following Hemispheric Deconnections", *Brain* 95 (1972).
25. Paula Broadwell and Vernon Loeb, *All In: The Education of David Petraeus* (New York: The Penguin Press, 2012).

Edwards Brothers Malloy
Thorofare, NJ USA
May 30, 2012